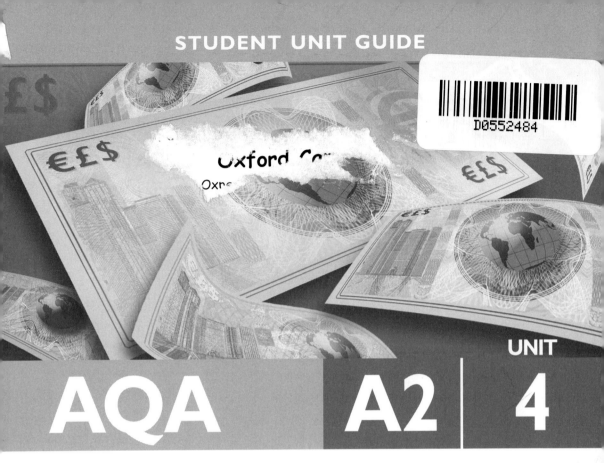

AQA

A2

UNIT
4

Economics

The National and International Economy

Ray Powell

Philip Allan Updates, an imprint of Hodder Education, an Hachette UK company, Market Place, Deddington, Oxfordshire OX15 0SE

Orders

Bookpoint Ltd, 130 Milton Park, Abingdon, Oxfordshire OX14 4SB
tel: 01235 827720
fax: 01235 400454
e-mail: uk.orders@bookpoint.co.uk
Lines are open 9.00 a.m.–5.00 p.m., Monday to Saturday, with a 24-hour message answering service. You can also order through the Philip Allan Updates website: www.philipallan.co.uk

© Philip Allan Updates 2010

ISBN 978-0-340-94746-3

First printed 2010
Impression number 5 4 3 2 1
Year 2014 2013 2012 2011 2010

This Guide has been written specifically to support students preparing for the AQA A2 Economics Unit 4 examination. The content has been neither approved nor endorsed by AQA and remains the sole responsibility of the author.

Typeset by Phoenix Photosetting, Chatham, Kent
Printed by MPG Books, Bodmin

Hachette UK's policy is to use papers that are natural, renewable and recyclable products and made from wood grown in sustainable forests. The logging and manufacturing processes are expected to conform to the environmental regulations of the country of origin.

Contents

Introduction

■ ■ ■

Content Guidance

■ ■ ■

Questions and Answers

Introduction

The aim of this guide is to prepare students for the AQA Advanced Level examination assessing A2 Unit 4: The National and International Economy. You should use the guide as follows:

(1) Read the introduction.

(2) The second and third sections of the book should then be used as supplements to other resources, such as class notes, textbooks, *Economic Review* and *AS/A-Level Economics Exam Revision Notes*. (The last two of these are published by Philip Allan Updates.) Because it contains summaries rather than in-depth coverage of all the topics in the specification, you should not use the guide as your sole learning resource during the main part of the course. However, you may well decide to use the guide as the main resource in your revision programme. You are strongly advised to make full use of the **Questions and Answers** section, especially in the revision period when you should be concentrating on improving your examination skills.

Examinable skills

The Unit examination is 2 hours long, has a maximum mark of 80 and contains two sections, Section A and Section B, which each count for 40 marks. There are two data-response questions (DRQs) in Section A, of which you should answer one. Question 1 is set on **the global context** and Question 2 is set on **the European Union context**. There are three essay questions (EQs) in Section B, of which you should answer one. There are no multiple-choice questions in either of the two A2 Unit examination papers.

The examination has four assessment objectives (AOs): knowledge; application; analysis; and evaluation, for which the requirements to achieve a grade A are set out in Table 1 (page 5).

In the A2 examination, 52% of the marks are awarded for lower-level skills and 48% for higher-level skills (with analysis and evaluation each accounting for 24%). This means the A2 Unit examinations are more difficult than the AS Unit exams, where only 40% of the total marks are awarded for the higher-level skills.

Data-response skills

Both the data-response questions in Section A of the Unit 4 exam paper contain three sub-questions. In the first exam in January 2010, the three sub-questions were listed as (a), (b) and (c). However, for later exams this has been changed to **(1)**, **(2)** and **(3)**. The mark allocation will be as follows: part (1): 5 marks; part (2): 10 marks; and part (3): 25 marks, which add to the total of 40 marks for the whole question. According to AQA, the change is being introduced to accommodate the needs of online marking.

Table 1 The four examination assessment objectives

	Assessment objective 1	Assessment objective 2	Assessment objective 3	Assessment objective 4
Assessment objectives	Demonstrate knowledge and understanding of the specified content	Apply knowledge and understanding of the specified content to problems and issues arising from both familiar and unfamiliar situations	Analyse economic problems and issues	Evaluate economic arguments and evidence, making informed judgements
A/B boundary performance descriptions	Candidates characteristically demonstrate across the AS and A2 specifications: a) detailed knowledge of a range of facts and concepts b) clear understanding of: • terminology • institutions • models c) detailed knowledge and clear understanding of the interconnections between the different elements of the subject content	Candidates characteristically apply clearly and effectively: • concepts numerical and graphical techniques • theories and models • terminology to complex issues arising in familiar and unfamiliar situations	Candidates characteristically: a) select relevant concepts, models, theories and techniques b) demonstrate, for the most part, development of logical explanations for complex economic problems and issues, with focus and relevance	Candidates characteristically evaluate effectively complex economic arguments: • prioritise evidence and arguments • make reasoned judgements • reach and present supported conclusions • make reasoned recommendations

The Unit 4 data-response questions contain slightly more data than AS data-response questions in the Unit 1 and 2 examinations. The layout and structure of the question will be similar to the six data-response questions in the Questions and Answers section of this guide. Each question is likely to contain two or three sets of data. With three data sets, the data will be labelled Extract A, Extract B and Extract C (for Question 1) and Extract D, Extract E and Extract F (for Question 2). One set of data is likely to be numerical, for example a line graph, a bar graph, a pie graph or a table. The other data set(s) will be text.

An 'incline of difficulty' will be built into each DRQ, with the earlier parts of the question being the most straightforward. Typically, the key instruction words for each part of the DRQ will be:

(1) Identify two points of comparison between…

(2) Explain (a term or concept) and then **analyse**…

(3) Evaluate (or possibly **assess** or **discuss**, or **do you agree?**, together with **justify your answer**)

Parts (1) and (2) of the questions will be marked using an **issue-based mark scheme** which lists the marks that can be awarded for the particular issues (and associated development) that might be included in the answer. Only lower-level skills (meeting AOs 1 and 2) are tested in part (1) of the questions. The higher-level skill of analysis is tested in parts (2) and (3) of the questions, but evaluation is only tested in part (3), where it accounts for 10 of the available 25 marks. Part (3) is marked using a **levels of response mark scheme**.

Part (3) of each DRQ differs from the earlier parts in three significant ways. First, and most obviously, it carries many more marks than parts (1) and (2) — 62.5% of the total marks for the question and 31.25% of the total marks for the whole paper. If you time the examination incorrectly and fail to develop your answer to part (3) beyond a cursory footnote, you will reduce considerably your chance of achieving a grade A, let alone an A*. Second, whereas parts (1) and (2) should be answered quite briefly, you are expected to write an extended answer of at least two pages for part (3). Think of this as a full-blown but nevertheless concise essay. Third, as I have already indicated, higher-level skills of **analysis** and particularly **evaluation** are expected for part (3).

A levels of response mark scheme containing five levels is used for part (3) of each DRQ and for part (2) of all the essay questions in Section B. (Numbered sub-questions are also being used in the essay questions, replacing parts (a) and (b).) You must familiarise yourself with the 'levels' mark scheme and bear it in mind when you practise the last part of data-response questions and essay questions. The key command word, e.g. to **evaluate** or **assess**, must be obeyed for your answer to reach the higher Level 4 and Level 5 standards of attainment set out in the levels of response mark scheme. Take special note of the summaries of each Level and the number of marks available for each Level. These are:

Level 1 A very weak answer (0–6 marks)

Level 2 A poor answer but some understanding is shown (7–11 marks)

Level 3 An adequate answer with some correct analysis but very limited evaluation (12–16 marks)

Level 4 Good analysis but limited evaluation (17–21 marks)

Level 5 Good analysis and evaluation (22–25 marks)

Your answer must evaluate the different arguments you set out, preferably as you make each argument. With many questions, discussion should centre on evaluating the advantages and disadvantages of (or the 'case for' versus the 'case against', or the costs and benefits of) a course of action mentioned in the question. Whether or not you have evaluated each argument as you make it, always try to finish your answer with a conclusion, the nature of which should vary according to the type of discussion or evaluation required. The conclusion might judge the relative strengths of the arguments discussed, possibly highlighting the most important argument. With many questions it is more appropriate to conclude whether, on balance, the case for is stronger than the case against and to provide some credible and reasoned justification for your opinion.

Essay-question skills

You must select *one* essay question from a choice of three when answering Section B of the paper. Your choice of question is obviously very important. Because the international economy accounts for approximately half the specification content, you should expect at least one essay question on international trade, patterns of UK or world trade, the balance of payments, exchange rates or globalisation.

Remember also that because of the global context and EU context nature of the data-response questions, international issues account for probably over half the total exam paper (though both data questions focus on the *impact* of an international issue on the UK economy).

The key instruction words for the two parts of each essay question are likely to be:

(1) Explain

(2) Evaluate (or possibly **assess** or **discuss**, or **do you agree?**, together with **justify your answer**)

As is the case with parts (1) and (2) of the data-response question, part (1) of the essay question tests the lower-level skills and assessment objectives of knowledge and application. The advice I have already given on how to answer part (3) of the data-response questions is equally applicable to answering part (2) of your chosen essay question.

The synoptic requirement of the Unit 4 examination

It is important to realise that the Unit 3 and Unit 4 examinations at A-level are **synoptic**. To understand what this means, you should compare the Unit 4 examination with the Unit 2 AS examination on The National Economy. Questions in the Unit 2 examination must only test knowledge and understanding of terms and concepts set out in the AQA Unit 2 specification. For example, a Unit 2 examination cannot contain a question on a macroeconomic issue which requires the candidate to apply a microeconomic concept (for example, elasticity) to explain a shift of the aggregate demand curve for the whole economy. Microeconomic demand and supply are in the Unit 1: Markets and Market Failure specification and not in the Unit 2 specification.

A question requiring the use of microeconomic theory to underpin macroeconomic theory could, however, appear in the Unit 4 examination. Such questions can illustrate both vertical synopticity and horizontal synopticity. **Horizontal**

synopticity requires the application of a Unit 3 microeconomic concept or theory (for example, poverty) to answer a Unit 4 macroeconomic question (for example, on the effects of fiscal policy). By contrast, **vertical synopticity** requires the use of AS macroeconomic concepts and theories (in the Unit 2 specification, such as the determinants of consumption) to answer Unit 4 macroeconomic questions on an issue such as the nature of a floating exchange rate.

Much of the coverage of macroeconomic theory in the Unit 4 specification is simply a *development* of what you learnt during your study of the Unit 2 course. At A2 there is little extra to learn about the determinants of the aggregate levels of output (and its rate of growth), employment, unemployment and average prices (and their rate of growth, i.e. the inflation rate). While there are some 'add-ons' (particularly Phillips curve analysis in the context of unemployment and inflation), the main difference between AS and A2 National Economy requirements lies in the greater sophistication of response needed to answer A2 data or essay questions. Put simply, the last parts of A2 exam questions require deeper and more extended answers than apparently similar AS questions. Your answers must show more knowledge of relevant recent economic events, analytical precision, and evaluation throughout the answer.

The major addition in Unit 4 to the content of the Unit 2 specification is of course **International Economics**. Trade theory was completely absent in Unit 2, apart from brief mentions of specialisation, division of labour and means of exchange. At AS you were expected to know about the balance of payments on current account, but not about international capital flows. Coverage of exchange rates was limited at AS, with no mention of the determinants and effects of floating and fixed exchange rates. The euro was not mentioned in the Unit 2 specification, nor was globalisation.

Checklist of relevant Unit 2 terms

- the meaning of national income and output, and its measurement: GDP
- understanding data in the form of index numbers and other forms of data presentation
- the distinction between nominal and real economic variables
- the objectives of a government's macroeconomic policy: full employment, growth, controlling inflation, a satisfactory balance of payments
- the economic cycle, booms, recessions, trend growth and actual growth, output gaps
- some of the main causes (types) of unemployment
- excess demand and rising costs as causes of inflation
- the role of monetary policy (interest rates) in controlling inflation
- the meaning of aggregate demand and aggregate supply
- using the *AD/AS* macroeconomic model to analyse events taking place in the economy, the level of economic activity and the effect of government intervention and policy

- components of aggregate demand and their effect on economic activity: consumption, investment, government spending and exports
- leakages or withdrawals of demand from the economy: saving, taxation and imports
- fiscal policy used both as a demand-side policy to manage aggregate demand and as a supply-side policy to improve the efficiency and competitiveness of markets and to shift the *LRAS* curve to the right
- supply-side policies to make labour and goods markets function more efficiently and competitively
- the current account of the balance of payments
- the effect of the exchange rate on the economy

Stretch and challenge and achieving the A* grade

The questions set in Unit 3 and Unit 4 examinations, offer you the opportunity of being 'stretched and challenged' in your responses to the questions you choose to answer. Stretch and challenge is designed to allow the brightest students the opportunity to demonstrate the full extent of their knowledge and skills.

According to AQA, the requirement to set questions in the Unit 3 and Unit 4 exams that stretch and challenge exam candidates is met by the parts of each of the data-response and essay questions that call for extended writing in the answers. These are part (3) of the data-response questions and part (2) of the essay questions. The higher skill levels (Levels 4 and 5) of the Levels mark scheme indicate the high expectations which candidates are required to meet in order to achieve high marks. The requirement for the questions set in the new A2 examination papers to stretch and challenge will be met by ensuring that mark schemes give due reward to candidates displaying the higher-level skills of analysis and evaluation in their answers to the last part of their chosen questions.

Achieving an A* grade

Stretch and challenge questions provide the opportunity to achieve an A* grade overall at A-level. Like the A* grade at GCSE, the A-Level A* grade attempts to address the need for greater differentiation between the most able and the slightly less able students. The most able students should gain an A* grade, while the slightly less able should achieve the standard A grade. Most importantly, a good performance at A2 is needed for an A* grade to be earned. A high mark at AS, accompanied by reasonable but not excellent performance at A2, may achieve an A grade, but not an A* in the overall A-level award that results from adding up the candidate's AS and A2 marks.

For A2 and A-level, the **Uniform Mark Scale (UMS)** needed to gain an A grade and an A* grade are shown in Table 2 (page 10). (The examiner who marks the exam paper awards a 'raw' mark, which is then converted into a UMS mark, for which the possible total mark per Unit exam is 100, with 80 being the grade boundary for grade A.)

Table 2 Uniform Mark Scale (UMS) requirements for grades A and A*

AS			A2	
	Maximum mark			Maximum mark
Unit 1	100	Unit 3		100
Unit 2	100	Unit 4		100
Total	200	Total		200
Grade A boundary	160	Grade A boundary	160	
	A-level (AS and A2)			
Total	400			
Grade A boundary	320			
A* requirement	320 overall, with 180 achieved at A2			

Revision planning

The revision strategy below is based on the use of this guide, supplemented by other resources such as the notes you have built up over your course of study and favoured textbooks. The programme is designed for the 3-week period before the examination. The strategy assumes you are revising at least two other A-level subjects (and for Unit 3: Business Economics and the Distribution of Income) during the same period, but are able to devote a session of 2 hours (plus half an hour for short breaks) to Unit 4 every other day, with shorter follow-up sessions on the intervening days. You should revise solidly for 6 days a week, but allow yourself 1 day off a week to recharge your batteries. The strategy can be modified to meet your personal needs and preferences: for example, by shortening each revision session and/or extending the sessions over a revision period longer than 3 weeks.

(1) Revise one topic from the Content Guidance section of this guide per revision session. Divide the revision session into four half-hour periods during which you are working solidly and without distraction, interspersed with 10-minute breaks.

(2) Proceed through the topics in the order they appear in the guide:
>   Week 1: Topics 1–3
>   Week 2: Topics 4–6
>   Week 3: Topics 7–9

(3) Vary the activities you undertake in each 30-minute period of a revision session. For example, spend the first 30 minutes reading through the Essential Information section of the topic. List key terms and concepts on a piece of paper. After a short break, use the second 30-minute period to check more fully the meaning of the key terms and concepts in your class notes and/or an economics textbook. Then after a second short break, check which essay questions and parts of data-response questions in the Questions and Answers section of the guide test aspects of the topic you are revising. Spend the rest of the 30 minutes answering some or all of the questions. In the final 30-minute period — or perhaps in a follow-up session a day or two later — carefully read through any candidate answers that relate to the parts of the essay question or DRQ covered by the topic, and also read the examiner's comments on the question(s) and answer(s).

To vary your revision programme, and to make sure you reinforce and retain the vital information revised in the longer sessions, you should fit some of the activities suggested below into follow-up sessions. Activities suitable for follow-up and 10-minute sessions include the following:

- Write definitions of some key terms and concepts relating to the topic revised on the previous day. Check each of your definitions against the correct definition in this guide, or in a textbook or your class notes.
- Draw key diagrams relating to the topic. Check any diagram you draw against a correct version of the diagram, making absolutely sure that the diagram is correctly and clearly labelled.
- Whenever you make mistakes, repeat these exercises every day or so, until you have eliminated all the mistakes.
- Answer questions from past AQA examination papers and from AQA's 'Specimen Units and Mark Schemes' booklet, which your teacher should have. Make sure your teacher obtains all the relevant June and January AQA past exam papers that are available at the time you take the examination. Identify and then answer questions from past papers that relate to the topic just revised. Then spend another follow-up session checking your answer(s) against the AQA mark scheme(s) to see how you could improve your answer(s).

Note: AQA now provides all its resources, including the specification, past exam papers and mark schemes, on its website: **www.aqa.org.uk**.

In addition, provided they are registered with e-AQA, your teachers can also access exam papers, mark schemes and examination reports rather earlier after the exams have finished. Any further information about AQA economics can be obtained from the Economics subject officer, AQA, Stag Hill House, Guildford, GU2 7XJ.

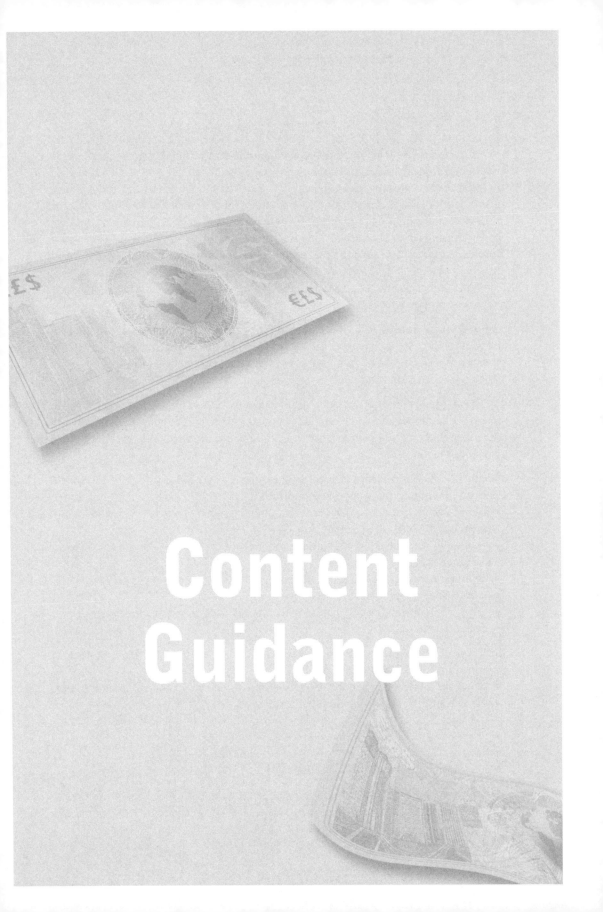

Content Guidance

In contrast to AS Unit 2: The National Economy, which is concerned with elementary macroeconomics, Unit 4: The National and International Economy centres for the most part on more advanced macroeconomics. As the specification states, Unit 4 builds on the knowledge and skills learnt in Unit 2. It requires candidates to use and evaluate more complex macroeconomic models than those introduced in Unit 2, and to develop further their critical approach to economic models and methods of enquiry. Nevertheless, you should be aware that, as in Unit 2, the **aggregate demand/aggregate supply (AD/AS) macroeconomic model** is the most important of all the models you need to know and to apply in your economic analysis. The *AD/AS* model is an essential part of the theoretical tool kit needed when analysing and evaluating the problems, puzzles or issues posed by a question.

Phillips curve analysis, both in the short run and the long run, is also required for answering Unit 4 examination questions. This is a completely new part of the specification which does not figure in Unit 2, except in the narrow sense of awareness of a conflict between macroeconomic objectives.

Unlike in Unit 2, and as the Unit title indicates, international economics is an important part of Unit 4. The main international topics you are expected to know are trade theory, the case for import controls, the balance of payments, exchange rates and globalisation.

Examples of issues which could be examined in the **global context** in the Unit 4 exam are the impact upon the UK economy of:
- externally generated demand-side economic shocks, such as recession in the USA, or Japan and the Far East
- externally generated supply-side economic shocks, such as the effect of global natural disasters
- changes in world trade and global patterns of trade
- World Trade Organization (WTO) decisions
- the global movement of capital affecting the UK balance of payments and exchange rate

Examples of issues in the **EU context** which could be examined in the Unit 4 exam are the impact upon the UK economy of:
- the EU as a trading bloc (customs union) and the Single European Market (SEM)
- the effect of the free movement of capital within the EU
- the single European currency (the euro) and the euro area (eurozone)
- Economic and Monetary Union (EMU)
- macroeconomic performance in other EU countries
- free movement of labour within the EU

The next section of the guide contains a summary of the AQA specification for Unit 4: The National and International Economy (pages 15–17), followed by notes about the nine topics of the specification (pages 17–62).

Introduction to the specification

The AQA specification for Unit 4 contains the following sections.

3.4.1 Macroeconomic indicators

Unit 2 introduced you to the economy's **actual growth rate** and its **trend growth rate**, and to the fluctuations around the trend rate of growth associated with the **economic cycle**. At A2 you must be able to apply at least two theoretical explanations of the economic cycle, although the specification is not prescriptive of what the explanations should be, apart from noting how **supply-side** or **demand-side shocks** can trigger cyclical fluctuations. Detailed theories of economic growth are *not* required.

It is necessary to understand the costs and benefits of economic growth, and the use and limitations of national income as an indicator of changes in living standards. You must be able to discuss the impact of growth on individuals and the environment. Knowledge of the sustainability of growth is needed, which implies an understanding of resource depletion and degradation.

You are expected to interpret different types of national income data, possibly for a range of countries, but you do not need to know technical details of national income accounts. You must be familiar with different types of data, such as the United Nation's Human Development Index, and to use them to compare living standards in different countries.

This section of the specification also builds on the knowledge acquired in Unit 2 on the **types** or **causes of unemployment** and **demand-side** (demand-pull) and **supply-side** (cost-push) **causes of inflation**. Both unemployment and inflation need to be analysed in the *AD/AS* theoretical framework. *AD/AS* needs to be understood in greater detail than in Unit 2, particularly with reference to the **natural rate of unemployment** and **Phillips curve analysis**. As with *AD/AS*, you must understand the difference between short-run and long-run Phillips curves. Neither **consumption** nor **investment** is mentioned in the Unit 4 specification, but along with the **national income multiplier**, they may be tested synoptically.

Along with other explanations of inflation, you must know the **quantity theory of money** as a special case of demand-pull inflation. The specification states that candidates should understand and evaluate the **monetarist model of inflation**, which implies some knowledge of the role of **expectations** in the inflationary process. You must also know how **index numbers** are calculated and used to **measure inflation**, and the effects of inflation on individuals and the performance of the economy.

3.4.2 Managing the national economy

The Unit 4 specification requires knowledge and understanding of **monetary policy**, **fiscal policy** and **supply-side policy** as three of the main ways of managing the national economy. You need to study all these in greater detail and with more rigour than for AS. You must also appreciate the **exchange rate** as a target and instrument of monetary policy, and the interrelationships between fiscal and monetary policy. You should understand the relationship between interest rates and the exchange rate and how the exchange rate influences policy objectives, such as inflation, unemployment and the balance of payments. Your knowledge of the conflicts between policy objectives should be more sophisticated at A2 than at AS.

Particular knowledge of the role of the **Monetary Policy Committee** of the Bank of England is required, especially in the context of its history of hitting or failing to hit the **inflation rate target** set by the government. Detailed knowledge of financial markets is *not* necessary, but you do need to understand that **bank deposits**, which are the main component of the money supply, are liabilities of the private enterprise banking system. Since it is unable to control bank deposits directly, the Bank of England attempts to influence monetary conditions via the effect of **interest rate changes** on the general public's desire to hold bank deposits. Detailed knowledge of the money supply is no longer required.

With regard to fiscal policy, the specification states the need for awareness of the introduction of **fiscal rules**. The specification was written before the suspension of the UK Code for Fiscal Stability in the recessionary conditions of 2008. However, knowledge of recent fiscal conditions is obviously needed, together with recent developments in monetary policy such as **quantitative easing**. Appreciation of the supply-side nature of much fiscal policy is also required, together with the demand-side use of fiscal policy, in the context of the government's budget, in the recent recession. Candidates must understand the canons of taxation and the microeconomic effects of changes in individual taxes.

3.4.3 The international economy

The international economy is covered in much greater depth in the Unit 4 specification than in the Unit 2 specification. Unit 4 requires knowledge of the **benefits of international trade** and the principle of **comparative advantage**, together with the possible costs of **international specialisation**.

Because of the 'context' format of the data-response questions, **globalisation** and the **European Union** are obviously important in this part of the specification. Globalisation should be given special attention via its effects, for good and for bad, on trade and the location decisions of multinational or transnational corporations. **Theories of protectionism** must be put into a European context related to the European Union as a **customs union**. Knowledge of the advantages and disadvantages of **Economic and Monetary Union (EMU)** and the **single European currency** (the **euro**) are also important.

Coverage of trade theory must include **patterns of trade** between the UK and the rest of the world. Some knowledge of the **capital account of the balance of payments** is also needed, but not in technical detail. However, the nature and significance of both **short-term** and **long-term international capital flows** should be understood. You must revise the current account of the balance of payments learnt for the AS course, and link current account deficits and surpluses to the exchange rate. Knowledge of both freely floating and fixed exchange rates is required, together with their links to interest rates and monetary policy and to domestic macroeconomic policy and conflicts.

The growth of modern macroeconomics

These notes, which relate to AQA specification sections 3.4.1 and 3.4.2, prepare you to answer AQA examination questions on:

- the approach of Keynesian and free-market economists to how the economy works
- the changing views of economists regarding the major objectives of macroeconomic policy

Essential information

The Keynesian revolution

These notes provide an overview of how macroeconomics has changed in recent economic history. More than any other individual, **John Maynard Keynes** created modern macroeconomics. Until monetarism in the 1970s, macroeconomics and **Keynesian economics** were much the same thing, growing out of Keynes's great and influential book, *The General Theory of Employment, Interest and Money*, published in 1936. Before Keynes, most economists belonged to the neo-classical or pre-Keynesian school (what is now called the free-market school). Pre-Keynesian economists believed that market forces operating in competitive markets provide a self-adjusting mechanism, which, in the long run, automatically ensures full employment and economic growth.

Figure 1 illustrates the pre-Keynesian explanation of employment and unemployment, in which full employment is determined at the level of employment where the aggregate demand for labour equals the aggregate supply of labour, at the wage W_{FE}. According to this theory, **classical** or **real-wage unemployment** is caused by wage rates being too high, at W_1 rather than W_{FE}.

Pre-Keynesians believed that real-wage unemployment is temporary. Market forces would cure the problem by bidding down wages until the number of workers willing to work equals the number that firms wish to hire. But in the 1930s, the market mechanism failed to cure unemployment. If an individual employer, or all the firms in a particular industry, cut wages in a single labour market within the economy, more workers are hired. Aggregate demand for output is little affected if the firm or industry is only a tiny part of the whole economy. But at the macro level, if real wages are cut throughout the economy, aggregate demand falls and firms cannot sell their output. Wage cuts may therefore increase rather than reduce unemployment.

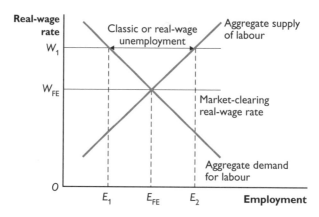

Figure 1 The pre-Keynesian theory of unemployment

Keynes argued that **deficient aggregate demand** causes unemployment. The paradox of thrift explains this. Saving, regarded as a virtue at the individual level, becomes a vice at the aggregate level if people save too much and spend too little. The policy solution is to inject demand back into the economy to counter the leakage of demand through saving. In its **fiscal policy**, the government should run a **budget deficit** (i.e. set $G > T$). In essence, the government borrows the excess savings of the private sector, which it spends itself, thereby injecting demand back into the economy and preventing the emergence of deficient demand.

The Keynesian era

The Keynesian era began shortly after 1945 when governments started to use demand management policies to achieve the objective of full employment. The era ended in the 1970s with the advent of monetarism and the free-market or new-classical revival. In the intervening 30 years governments in many industrial countries, including the United Kingdom, used fiscal policy to manage aggregate demand. When unemployment was high, the government expanded demand by increasing the budget deficit. As full employment was approached, increased demand caused imports to rise and the current account of the balance of payments to deteriorate. It also triggered **demand-pull inflation** since, in the short run at least, output could not rise to meet the increase in demand. A contractionary or deflationary policy of increased taxation and public spending cuts would be implemented. Macroeconomic policy in the Keynesian era was dominated by stop–go economics — successive periods of deflation and reflation resulting from the management of aggregate demand.

The crisis in Keynesian economics

For much of the Keynesian era, the policy of **fine-tuning** aggregate demand to a level consistent with full employment, but without excessive inflation, appeared to be working, and economic growth was more or less continuous. But at the same time, inflation began to creep up. Opponents of Keynesianism became more confident in their criticism of Keynesian theories and policies, arguing that Keynesian demand management could achieve full employment only through injecting greater and greater doses of inflation into the economy. Once achieved, full employment was becoming less and less sustainable.

By the mid-1970s Keynesianism was in disarray. Keynesian theory had been relatively invulnerable to serious attack as long as Keynesian economic management performed reasonably well when measured against the main objectives of economic policy: full employment, growth, control of inflation and a satisfactory balance of payments. Keynesianism became vulnerable to attack when a simultaneous failure to achieve any of the primary policy objectives occurred in the mid-1970s. The **stagflation** (slumpflation) of stagnant or declining output and growing unemployment combined with accelerating inflation, together with social conflict over the distribution of income and a deteriorating balance of payments, signalled the end of the Keynesian era.

The monetarist or free-market counter-revolution

The 1970s witnessed the decline of Keynesianism and the ascendancy of **monetarism**. Monetarists believe that the immediate cause of all inflation lies in a prior increase, permitted by governments, of the money supply.

Monetarism began in 1956 when Professor Milton Friedman revived the old pre-Keynesian theory of inflation, the **quantity theory of money**. The quantity theory argues that the quantity of money in the economy determines the price level and the rate of inflation. If the government allows the money supply to expand at a rate faster than the growth of output, the price level rises when people spend the excess money balances they hold.

Monetarist policies were implemented in the UK in the late 1970s and the early 1980s. The government abandoned discretionary demand management policies and based policy on automatic policy rules. The monetary policy rule centred on the publication of a target rate of growth of the money supply for a medium-term period of about 3 years ahead, accompanied by the announcement that monetary policy would be implemented to hit the money supply target. Other aspects of macro policy, including full employment as the major policy objective, were subordinated to the monetary policy aim of controlling monetary growth in order to achieve the new prime policy objective of controlling inflation. The government also adopted a fiscal policy rule based on reducing the size of public sector spending and borrowing as proportions of national output. Fiscal policy became subordinated to the needs of monetary policy, a situation that, except in the recent recession, still generally exists today.

The decline of monetarism and the growth of supply-side economics

Monetarism never really worked, with the growth in the money supply often outstripping the growth in prices. This unfortunate fact cast great doubt on the central assumption of narrow monetarism, namely that an increase in money supply causes inflation. But although the strictly 'monetarist' aspects of macroeconomic policy were quietly dropped after the mid-1980s, later UK governments have remained committed to the wider free-market aspects of economic policy adopted during the monetarist era. In particular, **supply-side economics** came to the fore, which aimed to improve the economy's supply side and its ability to produce.

Recent developments in macroeconomic policy

For several years before the onset of recession in 2008, monetary policy was again being used (via interest rate changes) to manage aggregate demand, but fiscal policy was used primarily as a supply-side policy, and not for managing aggregate demand. However, in the panic conditions induced by recession in 2008, for a short while at least, *both* policies were used to manage aggregate demand. In conditions of near-zero interest rates, further cuts in interest rates become ineffective as a means of stimulating aggregate demand. There are two reasons for this. First, as the bank rate is cut and falls close to zero, it becomes impossible to cut it below zero. Second, if the price level falls and deflation occurs, a zero *nominal* interest rate nevertheless means that *real* interest rates may remain quite high. In 2009, monetary policy switched briefly away from interest changes into a policy of **quantitative easing** (which is akin to printing more money in the hope that people will then spend it). At the same time, fiscal policy reverted to the Keynesian use of a growing budget deficit (called a **fiscal stimulus**) to pump spending into the economy. However, it was quickly realised that the resulting growth in government borrowing needed to finance the burgeoning deficit might be unsustainable. At the time of writing (December 2009), it is likely that swingeing public spending cuts will be introduced in 2010 to try to stem the rate of growth of government borrowing. However, a contractionary fiscal policy may nip in the bud recovery from recession, leading at worst to a 'double-dip' (W-shaped) recession, and at best to a stagnant economy with growing unemployment, even though output may no longer be falling.

Examination questions and skills

AQA economics examinations *do not* test knowledge of events more than about 10 years before the examination. Nevertheless, it is a good idea to possess such knowledge, if only to make better sense of current and very recent policies, and of events in the UK and world economies.

Common examination errors

- Failing to understand the major objectives of macroeconomic policy, and the ways in which their relative importance has changed.
- Confusing policy objectives and policy instruments.
- Treating Keynesianism and fiscal policy as interchangeable terms.
- Treating monetarism and monetary policy as interchangeable terms.
- Failing to appreciate the difference between discretionary economic policy and automatic policy rules.
- A lack of awareness of recent changes in methods used to manage the macroeconomy.

Economic growth, the economic cycle and living standards

These notes, which relate to AQA specification section 3.4.1, prepare you to answer AQA examination questions on:

- economic growth and the economic cycle
- the costs and benefits of economic growth
- national income and standards of living

Essential information

What you already know about economic growth and the economic cycle

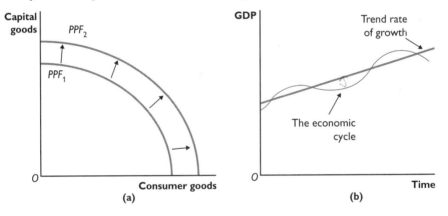

Figure 2 Aspects of economic growth

In your AS course, you learnt that **economic growth** can be defined as an increase in the economy's production potential. In panel (a) of Figure 2 this is illustrated by the outward movement of the **economy's production possibility frontier** from PPF_1 to PPF_2. (A rightward movement of the economy's long-run aggregate supply (*LRAS*) curve also illustrates economic growth.) By contrast, a movement from a point *inside* the frontier to a point on the frontier is called economic recovery, though some economists call this 'short-term economic growth'. Panel (b) shows the economy's trend rate of growth, together with its actual growth path depicted by the boom and recession of the **economic cycle**. The technical definition of a recession in the UK is if real output falls for 6 months or more. The economy's 'output gap', which measures the difference between the *actual* level of real output and the output that *would* be produced if the economy grew continuously at its trend rate, is another term you learnt at AS.

Economic growth

Economic growth results from investment in new capital goods (physical capital), which enlarges the national capital stock, and in human beings (human capital). But while investment is an important factor in the growth process, it may not be as important as technical progress. Until quite recently, economists had little to say about the causes of technical progress. However, an important new theory, known as **endogenous growth theory**, incorporates the causes of technical progress into the theoretical explanation of the growth process. The theory suggests that governments can create supply-side conditions that favour investment and technical progress. These conditions include external economies for businesses, often in the form of infrastructure, and a judicial system which protects patents and other intellectual property rights, and which enforces the law of contract.

Fluctuations in economic activity

Fluctuations in economic activity occur in three main ways: the economic cycle, seasonal fluctuations and a possible long cycle that lasts perhaps 60 years. Economic cycles, which are 4–12 years long, are caused primarily by fluctuations in aggregate demand (i.e. by shifts to the left and right of the *AD* curve). There are a number of different theories of the economic cycle and it is advisable to learn at least two theories in some depth. Examples include the following:

- Rapid growth produces a **speculative bubble** in asset prices (e.g. housing and/or shares), which rise far above the assets' real value. The bubble bursts, destroying consumer and/or business confidence. People stop spending and the economy falls into recession.
- The **political business cycle**. UK governments, which are elected at least every 5 years, may try to engineer a pre-election boom (to buy votes) and then deflate or contract the economy immediately after the election — until the next pre-election boom.
- Random **demand shocks** (and sometimes **supply shocks**) hit and throw the economy off course.

Seasonal fluctuations are related to climate (for example, very cold winters closing down the building trade). At the opposite extreme, long cycles of about 60 years have been identified. Significant improvements in technical progress (on the supply side of the economy) cause firms to invest in completely new technology, which triggers a long period of boom. Electrification and the automobile have had this effect. Around 2000, many economists believed that information and communication technology (ICT) was having a similar effect, possibly creating a **new economy**. However, the onset of recession in 2008 dampened this enthusiasm. In the past, long booms ran out of steam when the innovating technology became fully used — until, of course, the next burst of technical activity created another boom.

Stabilising the economic cycle

Demand management policies can be used to try to reduce fluctuations in the economic cycle. In the Keynesian era, fiscal policy was used in this way, but these days monetary policy is generally used to do this. In a boom when the economy is overheating, the Bank of England raises interest rates to contract or deflate aggregate demand. By contrast, in a recession the Bank of England cuts interest rates to reflate or boost aggregate demand. But successful stabilisation requires accurate timing.

Bad timing can destabilise the economic cycle and make it more volatile, and by causing long-term risky investments to be abandoned in favour of less risky short-term projects, unexpected interest rate (or tax) changes may affect competitiveness and long-term growth adversely.

The costs and benefits of economic growth

The ultimate purpose of economic activity is to improve economic welfare and people's standards of living. Economic growth can help to achieve this, but only if growth is compatible with economic development. Economic growth, which is *measured by* (though not *defined by*) the annual percentage growth in real national output, can have a number of costs that reduce economic welfare or happiness.

By contrast, **economic development**, which includes the quality and not just the quantity of growth, is measured by:

- a general improvement in living standards that reduces poverty and human suffering
- greater access to resources, such as food and housing, required for basic human needs
- greater access to opportunities for human development, e.g. through education and training
- environmental sustainability and regeneration, through reduced resource depletion and degradation

Resource depletion occurs when finite resources such as oil are used up, and when soil fertility or fish stocks decline irreversibly. By contrast, resource degradation is best illustrated by pollution of air, water and land. To benefit people in the long run, growth (and development) must be sustainable. **Sustainable economic growth** means the use of:

- renewable rather than non-renewable resources
- technologies that minimise pollution and other forms of resource degradation

The use and limitations of national income as an indicator of changes in living standards

When using national income figures to measure economic welfare, real national income per capita (or real GDP per capita) should be used to overcome the fact that prices rise and the population changes. Used in this way, national income figures provide quite a good estimate of the first two elements in the standard of living shown below:

| standard of living | = | economic welfare derived from goods and services purchased in the market economy | + | economic welfare derived from public goods and merit goods provided collectively by the state | + | economic welfare derived from quality of life factors, external benefits minus external costs or intangibles |

However, national income statistics both underestimate and overestimate economic welfare and living standards for the whole population. They *underestimate* activity because the non-monetised economy (such as housework and DIY) is under-represented, and because activity undertaken illegally in the hidden economy is omitted. The value of positive externalities shown in the third element of standards of living is also omitted from national income statistics. Improvements in the quality of goods may also be under-represented in national income statistics.

An important reason why national income statistics *overestimate* living standards and welfare relates to negative externalities such as pollution and congestion, and to activities such as crime. What is in effect a welfare loss may be shown as an increase in national output, falsely indicating an apparent welfare gain. For example, the stresses and strains of producing an ever-higher national output lead to a loss of leisure time and make people ill more often. Loss of leisure and poorer health are welfare losses. But in the national accounts, these show up as extra production and as extra consumption of healthcare, both of which imply a welfare gain. Likewise, installing 'regrettables' such as burglar alarms raises national income, but most people would prefer a crime-free environment and no burglar alarms. Significant disparity in income distribution also reduces the value of national income statistics as a measure of welfare. In developing countries the income distribution is typically extremely unequal and only a small fraction of the population may benefit materially from economic growth.

Comparing national income between countries

Comparisons of national income per head between countries are misleading if the relative importance of the non-monetised economy is significantly different. There are also differences in the degree of statistical sophistication in data collection, particularly between developed and developing countries, and a lack of international uniformity in methods of classifying and categorising national accounts. Further problems occur when making comparisons if different commodities are consumed. For example, expenditure on fuel, clothing and building materials is likely to be greater in developed countries with cold climates than in much warmer developing economies. But we must take care not to deduce from this single fact that greater expenditure — for example, on home heating — indicates higher real income and living standards.

A common method of comparing GNP per capita in different countries is to convert the GNP figures for each country into a common currency such as the US dollar. However, this calculation suffers from the assumption that the exchange rates between local currencies and the dollar are valued correctly, in the sense that a dollar's worth of output in one country becomes immediately and accurately comparable with a dollar's worth of output in any other country. This can never be so. Exchange rate changes only reflect the price changes of internationally traded goods. As there is a much wider gap in developing countries than in developed countries between the price changes of internationally traded and non-traded goods, GNP figures measured in US dollars tend to underestimate real levels of income and output in developing economies. The solution to this problem is to establish **purchasing power parity (PPP) exchange rates**, which means that a PPP dollar, or any PPP currency, buys the same quantity of a good everywhere in the world.

The **United Nations Human Development Index (HDI)** provides a better means of comparing welfare in different countries than national income or GDP statistics. The HDI combines measures of life expectancy, educational attainment and GDP per capita for all the world's countries and measures economic development rather than just national income.

Examination questions and skills

Examination questions which require detailed explanation of theories of growth are *not* likely to be set. You might, however, be asked to explain the causes of the economic cycle, possibly disguised in a question on the causes of fluctuations in economic activity. Alternatively, questions may centre on the *effects* (rather than the *causes*) of economic growth and/or cycles, for example focusing on the costs and benefits of economic growth.

Common examination errors
- Measuring economic growth in terms of the growth of nominal output rather than real output.
- Confusing economic growth with economic recovery.
- Confusing a cyclical upturn with the trend rate of economic growth.
- Failing to understand the difference between economic growth and economic development.
- Failing to understand sustainable economic growth, resource depletion and resource degradation.

Aggregate demand and aggregate supply

These notes, which relate to AQA specification section 3.4.2, prepare you to answer AQA examination questions on:
- understanding the nature of aggregate demand and aggregate supply
- applying the *AD/AS* model to analyse and evaluate problems and policy

Essential information

What you already know about aggregate demand and aggregate supply
The aggregate demand/aggregate supply (*AD/AS*) macroeconomic model, which is illustrated in Figure 3 (page 26), is just as important in Unit 4 as it is in Unit 2. You do not need to learn much more about *AD/AS* for the Unit 4 exam, but you are required to *apply* the model to explain, analyse and evaluate macroeconomic problems and policy in greater depth than for your AS course.

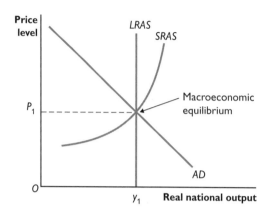

Figure 3 The AD/AS macroeconomic model

As in the AS course, the *AD/AS* macroeconomic model provides the theoretical framework that you are expected to use to analyse and evaluate economic problems and policy relating to economic growth, inflation and unemployment.

The **aggregate demand (AD)** curve in Figure 3 shows the total quantities of *real* output that all economic agents — households, firms, the government and the overseas sector — plan to purchase at different domestic price levels, when everything other than the price level is held constant. If any of the components of aggregate demand change, the curve will shift to the right or to the left, depending on the nature of the change. For example, an increase in consumer or business confidence shifts the *AD* curve to the right, via the effect on consumption or investment. Expansionary monetary and fiscal policy have a similar effect. By contrast, contractionary policy or a collapse in consumer or business confidence causes the *AD* curve to shift to the left.

You learnt in your AS course that there are two **aggregate supply (AS)** curves, an upward-sloping **short-run aggregate supply (SRAS)** curve and a vertical **long-run aggregate supply (LRAS)** curve. However, you did not learn much about *why AD* and *AS* curves have the shapes illustrated in Figure 3. The shapes of the curves, particularly the difference between the *SRAS* and the *LRAS* curves, are explained in the next section.

The aggregate demand (*A D*) curve

Two factors explain the *slope* of the *AD* curve, as distinct from a *shift* of the curve. The first is a wealth or real balance effect. Assuming a given nominal stock of money (or money supply) in the economy, a decrease in the price level increases people's real money balances, i.e. the same amount of money will now buy more. An increase in real money balances makes people feel wealthier, and since consumption is positively related to wealth, aggregate demand rises as the price level falls. The second effect follows from this. When the supply of any commodity (in this case, real money balances) increases relative to demand, its price falls. The rate of interest is the price of money; hence an increase in real money balances causes the rate of interest to fall, further stimulating consumption and investment spending.

Short-run aggregate supply (*SRAS*)

Just as the *AD* curve shows the total quantities of real output that economic agents plan to purchase at different price levels, so the *AS* curve shows the quantities of real output that businesses plan to produce and sell at different price levels. There are a number of possible shapes for the short-run *AS* (*SRAS*) curve. These different shapes carry different implications for macroeconomic policy.

Panel (a) in Figure 4 shows the inverted L-shaped *AS* curve, based on the Keynesian view of how the economy works, which was prevalent a generation ago. During the Keynesian era, it was widely believed that expansionary fiscal or monetary policy, which shifts the aggregate demand function from AD_1 to AD_2, reflates real output, which increases from y_1 to y_2, with the price level remaining unchanged at P_1. (The inverted L-shaped *AS* curve is sometimes called the *long-run* Keynesian *AS* curve, rather than cast as a short-run curve.)

The Keynesian view was that firms respond to increased demand by increasing output, without requiring an increase in the price level to persuade them to increase output or supply. But when full employment is reached, at real output level y_{FE}, a further increase in aggregate demand (for example, to AD_3) causes prices and not output to rise. Excess demand pulls up the price level to P_2 in a **demand-pull inflation**.

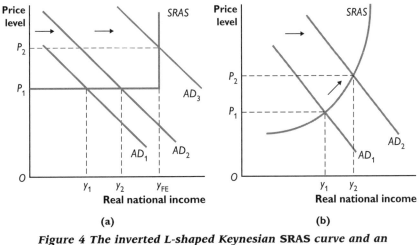

Figure 4 *The inverted L-shaped Keynesian* **SRAS** *curve and an upward-sloping* **SRAS** *curve*

Economists now generally reject the inverted L-shaped *AS* curve, believing instead that, in the short run at least, the *AS* curve slopes upwards as depicted in panel (b) of Figure 4. The upward-sloping *SRAS* curve stems from two important elements of microeconomic theory: the assumption that firms aim to maximise profit and the law of diminishing returns (diminishing marginal productivity). Following an expansion of aggregate demand from AD_1 to AD_2 in panel (b), which disturbs an initial macroeconomic equilibrium, the price level must rise to create conditions in which profit-maximising firms are willing to supply more output. To produce more output, more workers must be hired, but as they are hired, their marginal productivity falls and the marginal cost of production rises. When marginal costs rise, the prices charged by firms must also rise, otherwise it is not profitable to produce the extra output. The result is the upward-sloping short-run AS curve, which shows that a higher price level is required for firms to supply more output.

The vertical long-run aggregate supply ($LRAS$) curve

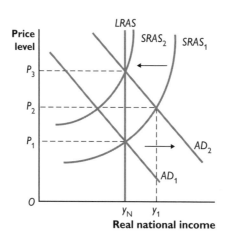

*Figure 5 The vertical **LRAS** curve*

A rise in the price level needed to increase $SRAS$ causes the real wage paid to workers to fall — providing money wage rates remain unchanged. What happens next depends on how workers respond to a real wage rate cut. There are two possibilities. If workers refuse to supply the extra labour needed to produce the extra output, income or output falls back to the equilibrium level of real output (y_N in Figure 5) prevailing before the shift to the right of the AD curve. But if workers respond to the higher price level by pushing up money wage rates to restore their real wage rates, then the short-run AS curve will shift to the left from $SRAS_1$ to $SRAS_2$ because costs of production have risen. As a result, the 'new' AD and AS curves (AD_2 and $SRAS_2$) once again intersect at the original equilibrium level of output y_N. For free-market economists, y_N is the natural level of output towards which market forces and a flexible price mechanism eventually adjust. It is the long-run equilibrium level of output associated with the natural levels of employment and unemployment of labour. The vertical line drawn in Figure 5 at the natural or equilibrium level of output is the long-run aggregate supply ($LRAS$) curve. The $LRAS$ curve carries the message that the short-run expansionary effect on output and employment, resulting from the government increasing aggregate demand beyond the economy's natural ability to produce additional output, is negated in the long run by the way the supply side of the economy responds to the demand stimulus.

The *AD/AS* model and economic policy

The *AD/AS* model is particularly useful for analysing the effect of an increase in aggregate demand on the economy because it addresses the important issue of whether expansionary fiscal policy and/or monetary policy will increase real output and jobs (i.e. **reflationary**), or whether the price level will increase instead (i.e. **inflationary**). In the short run, as has been explained, the answer to this key macroeconomic question depends on the shape of the *SRAS* curve, but in the long run, the vertical slope of the *LRAS* curve means that expanding aggregate demand to a level beyond y_N increases the price level but not real output.

The *LRAS* curve is located at the natural or equilibrium level of real output, which is the level of output consistent with the **natural rate of unemployment** in the labour market. Because output and employment are assumed to be at their natural or equilibrium levels, free-market economists conclude that it is generally irresponsible for governments to use expansionary fiscal or monetary policy to try to increase national output and employment. While such policies may succeed in the short run, though at the expense of inflation, they are doomed eventually to fail. In the long run, output and employment fall back to their equilibrium or natural levels, which are determined by the economy's production potential or ability to supply. Thus, instead of expanding demand to reduce unemployment *below* its natural rate, free-market economists believe that the government should use microeconomic supply-side policies to reduce the natural rate itself.

But if the economy is initially producing *below* y_N, there is a role for increasing aggregate demand to create the demand needed to absorb the economy's ability to supply more goods. However, as noted, increasing aggregate demand *beyond* y_N raises prices rather than output. (This analysis is relevant for evaluating the effect of the fiscal stimulus and the quantitative easing of the money supply, introduced to try to lead the UK economy out of recession in 2008 and after.)

Examination questions and skills

It is worth emphasising that the aggregate demand/aggregate supply (*AD/AS*) macroeconomic model is unlikely to be mentioned in a Unit 4 examination question, but that, as in the AS course, the model provides the main theoretical framework that you are expected to apply when analysing and evaluating macroeconomic problems and government policies. The *AD/AS* model can be used for analysing economic growth, employment and unemployment, inflation, and both demand-side and supply-side economic policy.

Common examination errors

- Confusing macroeconomic *AD* and *AS* curves with microeconomic demand and supply analysis.

- Mislabelling the axes of *AD/AS* diagrams.
- Confusing *AD/AS* diagrams with Phillips curve diagrams.
- Wasting time deriving *AD* or *AS* curves, instead of applying them to analyse the issue posed by the question.
- Failing to relate *AD/AS* diagrams to demand-side and supply-side economic policy.
- Failing to see the link between the natural level of real output in an *AD/AS* diagram and the natural rate of unemployment in a Phillips curve diagram.

Unemployment and inflation

These notes, which relate to AQA specification section 3.4.1, prepare you to answer AQA examination questions on the causes and consequences of:
- unemployment
- inflation

Essential information

What you already know about unemployment and inflation

When studying AS Unit 2: The National Economy, you learnt that there are two measures of unemployment in the UK. These are the **claimant count** and the **labour force survey (LFS)** measure. Likewise, you learnt that the **Retail Prices Index (RPI)** and the **Consumer Prices Index (CPI)** both measure the average price level, and from that the rate of inflation. You also learnt that full employment and unemployment can be illustrated on a production possibility frontier (*PPF*) diagram, and that there are two main causes of inflation: demand inflation (demand-pull) and cost inflation (cost-push).

In panel (a) of Figure 6 (page 31), full employment occurs at all points on the economy's *PPF*, such as *A* and *B*. By contrast, the distance from a point inside the frontier such as *C* to the frontier represents unemployment. In panel (b), a shift to the right of aggregate demand pulls up the price level (demand inflation). Panel (b) also illustrates cost-push inflation caused by a shift to the left of aggregate supply.

Who are the unemployed?

There are many people in the UK who are of working age and not working, but who are not 'officially' unemployed. These inactive people of working age include people who stay at home, students without a part-time job and those who retire early. In the early 2000s, the claimant count, which measures those who are unemployed and actually claiming benefit in the form of **jobseeker's allowance**, fell below 1 million, but the LFS measure, which includes the unemployed not claiming benefit, was about half a million higher. However, the onset of recession in 2008 caused unemployment to rise to 2.46 million by September 2009 measured by the LFS, and to 1.64 million measured by the claimant count.

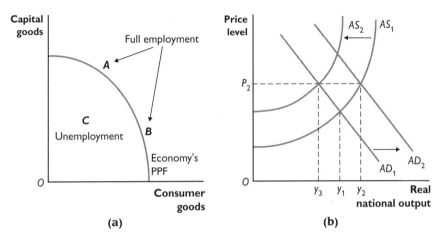

Figure 6 Full employment, unemployment and the causes of inflation

The causes of unemployment

Before Keynes, the **classical** or **real-wage theory of unemployment** (explained on page 17) was the dominant theory of unemployment. Other types or causes of unemployment are **frictional**, **structural** and **demand-deficient**.

Frictional and structural unemployment

In a dynamic economy, change takes place constantly, with some industries declining and others growing. As new products are developed and demand and cost conditions change, firms demand more of some labour skills while the demand for other types of labour declines. Economists use the terms frictional and structural unemployment to describe the resulting unemployment. Frictional unemployment, as its name suggests, results from frictions in the labour market that create a delay or time-lag during which a worker is unemployed when moving from one job to another. Because there will always be some frictional unemployment, even when there is 'full employment', frictional unemployment is also called **equilibrium unemployment**. Some frictional unemployment can be explained by the search theory of unemployment. Suppose that a worker earning £600 a week in a skilled occupation loses her job. There are plenty of vacancies for unskilled workers, at much lower wage rates, but none at £600. In this situation, the worker chooses to remain voluntarily frictionally unemployed, partly because the wage and working conditions do not meet her aspirations, and partly because better-paid vacancies exist which she does not, as yet, know about, but which may be discovered through actively searching the labour market.

Structural unemployment results from the structural decline of industries unable to compete or adapt in the face of either changing demand and new products, or changing ways of producing existing products and the emergence of more efficient competitors in other countries. The growth of international competition has been a particularly important cause of structural unemployment. **Technological**

unemployment is a special case of structural unemployment resulting from the successful growth of new industries using labour-saving technology such as automation.

Keynesian or demand-deficient unemployment

Keynes believed that deficient aggregate demand was a major cause of persistent mass unemployment. One of the main disputes separating Keynesian and free-market economists centres on the nature of demand-deficient unemployment. Economists generally agree that **temporary unemployment** (called **cyclical unemployment**) may be caused by a lack of demand in the downswing of the economic cycle. However, Keynes went further, arguing that the economy could settle into an under-full employment equilibrium caused by a continuing lack of effective aggregate demand. As the sections on monetary policy and fiscal policy explain (pages 40–45 and 45–50) Keynesian economists believe that governments should actively manage the level of aggregate demand to reduce or eliminate demand-deficient unemployment. In recent years, the 2008 recession led to renewed interest in what Keynes had to say more than 70 years ago about how a lack of aggregate demand may lead to mass unemployment.

The consequences of unemployment

Unemployment represents a waste of human capital. Nevertheless, free-market economists believe that a certain amount of unemployment is necessary to make the economy function better. By providing downward pressure on wage rates, unemployment may reduce inflationary pressures. However, it tends to widen income differentials and increase absolute and relative poverty. Higher unemployment means greater spending on unemployment and poverty-related benefits, the opportunity cost of which is less spending on the provision of hospitals, schools and other useful resources.

Governments generally implement policies to try to reduce unemployment, but the appropriate policy obviously depends on identifying the underlying cause of unemployment correctly. For example, if unemployment is diagnosed in terms of demand deficiency, when the 'true' cause is structural, a policy of fiscal or monetary expansion to stimulate aggregate demand will be ineffective and inappropriate. Indeed, reflation of demand in such circumstances would probably create excess demand, which would raise the price level in a demand-pull inflation, with no lasting beneficial effects on employment.

Despite the recent recession, it is now widely agreed, by Keynesians as well as by free-market economists, that the cause of long-term unemployment in countries such as the UK lies on the supply side of the economy rather than on the demand side. There is much disagreement, however, on the appropriate policies to improve supply-side performance. Free-market economists argue that poor supply-side performance is the legacy of decades of Keynesian interventionism a generation or more ago. To cut frictional, structural and real-wage unemployment, the economic role of the state must be reduced rather than extended. By setting markets free, encouraging competition and fostering private enterprise and the entrepreneurial spirit, an enterprise culture can be created in which the price mechanism, and not the government, will deliver economic growth and reduce unemployment. In the free-market view, the correct role of government is to create the conditions, through controlling inflation, promoting competitive markets and maintaining the rule of law and social order, in which the market mechanism and private enterprise can function properly. Many modern Keynesians disagree, arguing (using evidence provided by the recent recession) that unemployment results from a massive market failure, which can only be cured by interventionist policies to modify the market and make it function better.

The causes of inflation: demand-pull and cost-push inflation

Inflation is defined as a persistent or continuous rise in the price level, or as a fall in the value of money. Demand-pull inflation is caused by excess demand in the economy pulling up the price level. The quantity theory of money (which is at the heart of monetarist economic theory) is the oldest theory of demand-pull inflation. According to the quantity theory, the government creates or condones an expansion of the money supply greater than the increase in real national output. As a result, households and firms hold excess money balances which, when spent, pull up the price level — given the fact that real output cannot expand in line with the increase in spending power.

The quantity theory of money can be developed from the **equation of exchange**:

money supply $\times$ velocity of $=$ price level $\times$ total transactions
(or stock of   circulation   in the economy
money)   of money

$$\text{or: } MV = PT$$

For an increase in the money supply (on the left-hand side of the equation) to pull up the price level (on the right-hand side), the velocity of circulation of money (how often money is spent) and total transactions (an indicator of real national income) must both be constant, or at least stable. Keynesians do not accept these monetarist assumptions. As a result, the quantity theory of money and the causes of inflation form a major area of dispute between Keynesian and free-market economists.

Arguing that governments condone excessive increases in the money supply, monetarists blame governments for inflation. By contrast, Keynesian theories of demand-pull inflation generally ignore the money supply and locate the cause of inflation in the factors that increase consumer spending and borrowing, and in the tendency of governments to increase public spending and budget deficits (in fiscal policy) in order to win elections.

Many Keynesians favour the cost-push theory of inflation, which can be illustrated by a shift to the left of the short-run *AS* curve. Until recently, cost-push theory located the cause of inflation in trade union activity and in other causes of market imperfection in both the product market and the labour market. In labour markets, their strength enables trade unions to bargain for money wage increases in excess of any rise in labour productivity. Monopoly firms pay these wage increases, partly because of the costs of disrupting production and partly because they believe that they can pass on the increasing costs as price rises. Cost-push theories usually assume that wages are determined through the process of collective bargaining, while in the goods market, prices are formed by a cost-plus pricing rule through which monopolistic firms add a standard profit margin to their costs when setting prices. Thus trade union militancy and big businesses' monopoly power were blamed for inflation. In recent years, with the decline of trade union power and militancy, external economic shocks, for example resulting from a sudden rise in the world price of oil, have been blamed for triggering cost-push inflation, though arguably the underlying cause of these shocks lies in excess global demand for scarce commodities.

The consequences of inflation

Everybody agrees that inflation can have serious adverse effects or costs. However, the seriousness of the adverse effects depends on whether inflation is anticipated or unanticipated. If inflation could be anticipated with complete certainty, it would pose few problems. Households and firms would simply build the expected rate of inflation into their economic decisions, which would not be distorted by wrong guesses. When inflation is relatively low, with little variation from year to year, it is easy to anticipate next year's inflation rate. Creeping inflation can be associated with growing markets, healthy profits and a general climate of business optimism, greasing the wheels of the economy. Indeed, a low rate of inflation may be a necessary cost of expansionary policies to reduce unemployment. But some free-market economists argue that inflation acts like sand in the wheels of the economy, making it less efficient and competitive. If the sand-in-the-wheels effect is stronger than the greasing-the-wheels effect, the costs of inflation exceed the benefits.

Particular consequences of inflation are as follows:
- **Distributional effects.** Weaker social groups in society on fixed incomes lose, while those in strong bargaining positions gain. Also, with rapid inflation, real rates of interest may be negative. In this situation, lenders are really paying borrowers for the doubtful privilege of lending to them, and inflation acts as a hidden tax, redistributing income and wealth from lenders to borrowers.
- **Distortion of normal economic behaviour.** Inflation can distort consumer behaviour by causing households to bring forward purchases and hoard goods if they expect the rate of inflation to accelerate. Similarly, firms may divert funds out of productive investment in fixed investment projects into unproductive commodity hoarding and speculation.
- **Breakdown in the functions of money.** In a severe inflation, money becomes less useful and efficient as a medium of exchange and store of value. Rapidly changing prices also erode money's functions as a unit of account and standard of deferred payment. In a hyperinflation, less efficient barter replaces the use of money and imposes extra costs on most transactions.
- **International uncompetitiveness.** When inflation is higher than in competitor countries, exports increase in price, putting pressure on a fixed exchange rate.

With a floating exchange rate, the exchange rate falls to restore competitiveness, but rising import prices may fuel a further bout of inflation.

- **Shoe leather and menu costs.** Consumers incur shoe leather costs, spending time and effort shopping around and checking which prices have or have not risen. By contrast, menu costs are incurred by firms, having to adjust price lists more often.

Examination questions and skills

Examination questions are likely to cover the causes of unemployment and inflation, interrelationships between the two (see the next section), and application of *AD/AS* theory to explain the causes of unemployment and inflation, the costs and benefits of inflation, and how economic policy might reduce unemployment or inflation.

In recent years, the fear of deflation (continuously *falling* prices) has to some extent replaced the fear of inflation and continuously *rising* prices. Examination questions are likely to reflect this, together with the accompanying recessionary conditions that may lead to deflation of the price level.

Common examination errors

- Assuming that full employment means that everybody is employed.
- Failing to understand the difference between and the adequacy of the two ways of measuring unemployment.
- Confusing frictional and structural unemployment.
- Writing about relatively trivial causes of unemployment, such as seasonal and casual unemployment, when the question is about the more important frictional, structural and demand-deficient causes.
- Confusing inflation with a one-off price change, or with relative price changes.
- Failing to appreciate conflicts between full employment and price stability as macroeconomic policy objectives (see the next topic).
- Assuming that inflation is always bad and never good, and that deflation must be good because inflation is bad.
- Failing to understand how price indices such as the CPI measure inflation.

The Phillips curve and the natural rate of unemployment

These notes, which relate to AQA specification section 3.4.1, prepare you to answer AQA examination questions on:

- the short-run and the long-run Phillips curve
- factors determining the natural rate of unemployment (NRU)
- the implications of the Phillips curve and the NRU for economic policy

Essential information

What you already know about the Phillips curve and the natural rate of unemployment

At AS, you learnt about the conflict between full employment and controlling inflation, as macroeconomic policy objectives. However, the Unit 2 specification makes no mention of the Phillips curve or of the natural rate of unemployment.

The original (short-run) Phillips curve

At the height of the Keynesian era two generations ago in the 1950s, A. W. Phillips argued that a stable inverse statistical relationship exists between the rate of *wage* inflation and the percentage of the labour force unemployed. (More usually these days, the Phillips curve measures the inverse relationship between unemployment and the rate of *price* inflation.)

The Phillips curve is *not* a theory of inflation, but it gives support to both the main theories of inflation. In the demand-pull theory, falling unemployment is associated with excess demand, which pulls up wages and prices. In the cost-push theory, falling unemployment increases the market power of workers in the labour market, enabling them to push for higher wages.

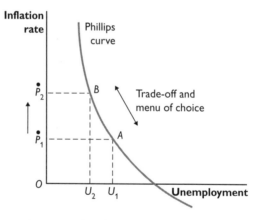

Figure 7 The short-run Phillips curve

Although the Phillips curve illustrates the conflict between full employment and control of inflation as policy objectives, it also suggests how the conflict can be dealt with. Suppose unemployment is initially U_1 and the rate of inflation is $\dot{P}_1$, with the economy at point A on the Phillips curve. By increasing aggregate demand, the government can move the economy to point B. Unemployment falls to U_2, but at the cost of a higher rate of inflation at $\dot{P}_2$.

The breakdown of the Phillips relationship

The Phillips curve indicates that by using demand management policies, governments can trade off between the number of jobs in the economy and the rate of inflation. Points such as A and B on the Phillips curve represent a menu of choice from which governments can choose when deciding an acceptable combination of unemployment and inflation. But in the 1970s, accelerating inflation and growing unemployment occurred together. The breakdown of the Phillips curve relationship was a major cause of the free-market counter-revolution that replaced Keynesianism.

The long-run Phillips curve ($LRPC$) and the natural rate of unemployment (NRU)

Economists now generally recognise that the Phillips curve in Figure 7 is a short-run Phillips curve ($SRPC$), representing the *short-run* relationship between inflation and unemployment. In Figure 8(a), a vertical long-run Phillips curve ($LRPC$) has been added to the diagram, cutting the short-run Phillips curve where the rate of inflation is zero. The rate of unemployment at this point is called the **natural rate of unemployment (NRU)**, depicted by the symbol U_N.

Free-market economists believe that it is impossible to reduce unemployment below the NRU, except at the cost of suffering an ever-accelerating inflation, which, by eventually accelerating into a hyperinflation, eventually destroys the economy. They argue that the original, Keynesian, explanation of the (short-run) Phillips curve wrongly took into account only the *current* rate of inflation, and ignored the important influence of the *expected* rate of inflation. Figure 8(b) shows what happens when the role of expectations is brought into the Phillips curve diagram.

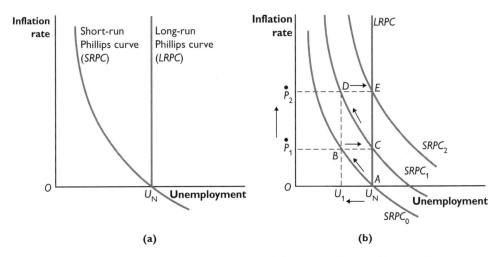

(a)   (b)

Figure 8 The long-run Phillips curve and the natural rate of unemployment

Let us assume that the rate of growth of labour productivity is zero and that the rate of *price* inflation equals the rate of *wage* inflation. The economy is initially at point A, with unemployment at the natural rate U_N. At point A, the rate of inflation is zero, as is the rate of increase of money wages. Let us also assume that people form their expectations of *future* inflation in the next time period solely on the basis of the *current* rate of inflation. At point A, current inflation is zero, so workers expect the future rate of inflation also to be zero.

Suppose the government increases aggregate demand, to trade off along Phillips curve $SRPC_0$ to a point such as B, where unemployment at U_1 is below the natural rate, U_N. Inflation initially rises to $\dot{P}_1$ or 5%. But a point such as B is unsustainable. This is because, for workers to supply more labour, the real wage must rise, yet a rising real wage causes employers to demand less labour. In the short run, more workers may indeed enter the labour market in the false belief that a 5% increase in *money* wages is also a *real* wage increase. This is called money illusion. Similarly, firms may be willing to employ more labour if they also suffer money illusion, believing falsely that rising prices mean that sales revenues are rising faster than labour costs.

To sustain an increase in employment *above* the natural rate (and to reduce unemployment *below* the NRU), workers and employers must suffer permanent money illusion in equal but opposite directions to keep expectations of inflation, formed in the previous time period, consistently below the actual rate to which inflation has risen. But workers continuously adjust their expectations of future inflation to the rising actual rate and bargain for ever-higher money wages to restore the real wage to the level necessary to reduce unemployment below U_N. As they do this, the short-run Phillips curve shifts outwards from $SRPC_0$ to $SRPC_1$ and so on. There is a separate short-run Phillips curve for each expected rate of inflation. Further out short-run Phillips curves such as $SRPC_1$ and $SRPC_2$ are associated with higher expected rates of future inflation. Conversely, the short-run Phillips curve shifts inwards when the expected rate of inflation falls.

Free-market economists argue that, in the long run, the only way to keep unemployment *below* the NRU is to permit the money supply to increase so as to finance an ever-accelerating inflation. For this to happen, inflation has to accelerate above the rate that workers and firms are expecting, for example from $\dot{P}_1$ to $\dot{P}_2$. But, as noted earlier, an accelerating inflation will eventually create a hyperinflation, which, in the resulting breakdown of economic activity, will almost certainly increase the NRU. Any attempt to reduce unemployment below the NRU is therefore foolhardy and irresponsible. In the short run it accelerates inflation, while in the long run it perversely increases the NRU to an unnecessarily high level.

If the government realises that it made a mistake initially when expanding the economy to point B, it can stabilise the rate of inflation at 5%. Workers and employers see through their earlier money illusion and realise that they have confused money quantities with real quantities. They refuse respectively to supply, and to demand, the labour necessary to keep unemployment below the NRU. The economy then moves to point C in Figure 8(b). Once point C is reached, any further increase in aggregate demand would move the economy to point D and an inflation rate of $\dot{P}_2$ — and to a repeat of the process just described, but starting from a higher initial rate of inflation.

Adaptive expectations versus rational expectations
The theory just described is based on the **theory of adaptive expectations**, in which workers and firms form expectations of what will happen in the *future* only on

the basis of what is happening *currently* and upon what has happened in the *recent* past. However, new-classical economists favour an alternative theory of how expectations are formed, called the **theory of rational expectations**. According to this theory, it is unrealistic to assume that workers and firms, acting rationally in their self-interest, form expectations of future inflation *solely* on the basis of current or recent inflation. If they can forecast the results of events taking place in the economy now, self-interest dictates that they should quickly modify their economic behaviour to take account of the most up-to-date information available. New-classical economists reject the idea that economic agents suffer money illusion for quite long periods — a vital component in the explanation of the short-run Phillips curve. If expectations are formed *rationally* rather than *adaptively*, any attempt by a government to reduce unemployment below its natural rate by increasing aggregate demand fails, leading solely to accelerating inflation. The correct way to reduce unemployment is to reduce the natural level itself, rather than to expand demand to try to reduce unemployment below the NRU. To do this, the government should use appropriate free-market supply-side policies.

Supply-side policy and the natural rate of unemployment

Figure 9 shows how supply-side policy, in the form of business and income tax cuts, can shift the long-run Phillips curve to the left and reduce the NRU. A cut in business

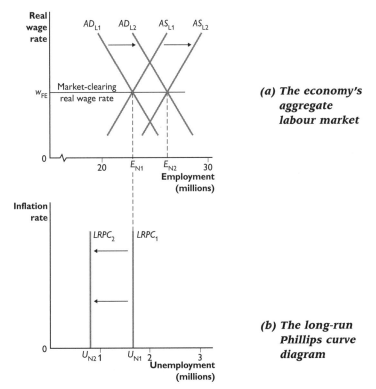

(a) *The economy's aggregate labour market*

(b) *The long-run Phillips curve diagram*

Figure 9 Supply-side policies increasing the natural level of employment and reducing the natural level of unemployment

taxation reduces costs of production, thereby shifting the aggregate demand curve for labour (shown in panel (a)) from AD_{L1} to AD_{L2}. Likewise, income tax cuts granted to workers shift the aggregate supply curve of labour from AS_{L1} to AS_{L2}. As a result, the natural level of employment in the aggregate labour market increases from E_{N1} to E_{N2}. This in turn reduces frictional unemployment (and the NRU) in panel (b) of the diagram, shifting the long-run Phillips curve to the left from $LRPC_1$ to $LRPC_2$. The NRU thus falls from U_{N1} to U_{N2}.

Examination questions and skills

Whereas an AS question is likely to ask about the *causes* of unemployment and inflation, an A2 question could also test understanding of the *conflicts* and *trade-offs* between full employment and control of inflation. Questions might mention the Phillips curve, but they are likely to leave it to you to distinguish between the short-run and long-run Phillips curves and to apply them as analytical tools. Likewise, the natural rate of unemployment is a key analytical concept that may or may not be mentioned in a question. It is important to use the NRU when explaining and evaluating the significance of both demand-side and supply-side economic policies.

Common examination errors

- Confusing short-run and long-run Phillips curves.
- Confusing Phillips curve diagrams with *AD/AS* diagrams.
- Confusing a reduction of unemployment *below* the NRU with a *shift to the left* of the NRU.
- Failing to relate the NRU to the analysis of supply-side economic policy.
- Failing to relate NRU analysis to the functioning of the aggregate labour market.

Monetary policy

These notes, which relate to AQA specification section 3.4.2, prepare you to answer AQA examination questions on:
- the instruments and objectives of monetary policy
- the role of the Bank of England in implementing monetary policy in the UK
- the link between financial markets and monetary policy

Essential information

What you already know about monetary policy

In your AS course, you learnt that monetary policy attempts to achieve the policy objectives set by the government using monetary instruments such as interest rates and controls on bank lending. You also learnt that the Bank of England, the country's central bank, raises or lowers interest rates, and that this shifts the *AD* curve to the left or to the right in the *AD/AS* macroeconomic model, thereby affecting output, employment and the rate of inflation.

Money and monetary policy

Money is best defined by the two main functions it performs in the economy, as a **medium of exchange** and as a **store of value** or **wealth**. **Cash** and **bank deposits** are the two main forms of money. Cash is really just the small change of the monetary system. Bank deposits, which are liabilities of the private enterprise banking system, are by far the major part of modern money. For the most part, at least until the introduction of the emergency policy of **quantitative easing** to fight recession in 2009, monetary policy has centred on the Bank of England raising or lowering its own interest rate (**bank rate**), to control or influence the ability of the commercial banks to create deposits when they lend to customers.

When implementing monetary policy, the Bank of England controls the supply of cash to the banking system. However, the Bank of England always issues enough cash to enable the commercial banks to meet customer demand for cash, thereby maintaining confidence in the banking system. By being always willing to supply cash in this way, the Bank of England acts as **lender of last resort** to the banking system. Supplementing interest rate policy, quantitative easing was introduced in 2009 as a temporary measure to increase the amount of cash supplied to the banking system. The Bank of England hoped that, being awash with cash, high street banks would lend more to the general public to get the economy out of recession. By the time you read this guide, quantitative easing may well have ended, in which case interest rates will once again be the main, and possibly the only, monetary policy instrument.

Monetarism

For a fairly short period from the late 1970s until the mid-1980s, UK monetary policy was **monetarist**. Monetarists are so called because they believe that inflation is caused by prior excess growth of the money supply, via the **quantity theory of money**. They also believe, first, that control of inflation should be the government's main policy objective and, second, that to control inflation the rate of growth of the money supply must be strictly controlled. But in the short-lived monetarist experiment, monetarist policies did not work, and UK monetary policy ceased to be monetarist after the mid-1980s. However, two important features of monetarist monetary policy have survived. First, monetarists disliked unnecessary government intervention in the economy and therefore abandoned the controls on bank lending used by the Keynesians. Second, control of inflation has continued through the 1990s and early 2000s to be the ultimate objective of UK monetary policy.

The framework of UK monetary policy

The framework of current UK monetary policy was created by a Conservative government in 1992, modified by the incoming Labour government in 1997, and given a few minor changes when the decision was made not to join the euro (at least for the time being) in 2003. Before 1997, the monetary authorities who implemented monetary policy were the Chancellor of the Exchequer (in charge of the Treasury) and the Governor of the Bank of England. The authorities raised or lowered interest rates to try to keep the inflation rate below a target rate set by the government. The policy had a **deflationary bias**, since the further inflation fell below the target rate, the greater the deemed success of monetary policy.

In 1997, the Labour government reformed the monetary policy framework, primarily by making the Bank of England operationally independent in implementing policy to hit the inflation rate target set by the government, and by establishing the **Monetary Policy Committee (MPC)** to formulate and undertake policy to achieve this goal. The Labour government's monetary policy should be regarded as a reform of the policy inherited from the Conservatives, rather than as a root-and-branch upheaval. The following features, which pre-date May 1997, continue as essential elements of the current policy:

- Monetary policy is implemented to hit an inflation rate target set by the government. The policy instrument used to achieve this is the Bank of England's official interest rate (bank rate), a change in which affects other short-term interest rates. This is partly through an 'announcement effect', and partly through the Bank of England's intervention in financial markets, which massages other short-term interest rates in the direction of the official rate.
- The inflation rate target is now symmetrical. Prior to May 1997, monetary policy aimed to get the inflation rate on or below the target rate set by the government and, as noted, the policy had an in-built deflationary bias. Arguably, this is no longer the case. The MPC is now prepared to reduce interest rates to stimulate output and employment if it believes that, on unchanged policies, an inflation rate below the target rate will be accompanied by an undesirable fall in output and employment. In the government's words: 'the primary objective of monetary policy is price stability, but subject to that, the Bank of England must also support the government's economic policy objectives, including those for growth and employment.'
- The money supply and the exchange rate are now used as indicators of whether monetary policy is on course to achieve the 2% inflation rate target.
- Monetary policy is pre-emptive. Policy makers at the Bank of England estimate what the inflation rate is likely to be 18 months to 2 years ahead (the medium term) if policy (that is, interest rates) remains unchanged. If the forecast rate of inflation is too far away from the target rate set by the government, the Bank is prepared to change interest rates immediately to prevent the forecast inflation rate becoming a reality. The Bank is also prepared to raise or lower interest rates to pre-empt any likely adverse effects on the inflation rate of an outside shock hitting the economy. Such a shock can justify a sudden change in interest rates to meet the unforeseen danger caused by the shock.

Supporters claim that the new monetary policy is transparent and accountable, and that the MPC is subject to parliamentary scrutiny. If inflation strays more than 1 percentage point higher or lower than the official target, the open letter system requires that the Governor of the Bank of England write to the Chancellor of the Exchequer, explaining why the divergence has occurred. Any such letter must be published to promote transparency. Until the introduction of a fiscal stimulus in the recessionary conditions of 2008, monetary policy (but not fiscal policy) was being used to manage the level of aggregate demand, to some extent in the old Keynesian style. However, an independent MPC, unless leaned on by the government, is unlikely to engineer an inflationary pre-election boom as in the old 'political business cycle' of the Keynesian era. By the time you read this guide, the fiscal stimulus will probably have been abandoned, and the new government elected in 2010 may also have changed the nature of monetary policy once again.

Evaluating the success of UK monetary policy

Before the 2008 recession and the introduction of quantitative easing in 2009, the success of UK monetary policy was measured by the extent to which the inflation rate target set by the government had been met as a result of interest rates set by the Bank of England. Judged in this way, monetary policy was usually extremely successful. The rate of inflation measured by the CPI almost always lay been between 1% above or below the 2% target. Just before the onset of recession in 2008, a burst of cost-push inflation caused by rapidly rising oil and commodity prices meant that inflation temporarily breached the 3% upper limit. However, this was quickly followed by the inflation rate falling, indeed becoming negative (**deflation**) when measured against changes in the RPI. The falling average price level (measured by the fall in RPI) accompanied the recession. Quantitative easing was introduced in 2009 to try to pump new money into the banking system, in the hope that the banks would lend the newly created money to the general public, who would then spend the economy out of recession.

Money and financial markets

Everyone, except the destitute, makes decisions on the form of asset in which to keep wealth (an asset is anything that has value). First, people choose between physical assets such as houses (which provide a good hedge against inflation) and financial assets. Second, they choose the form of financial asset to hold. Figure 10 (page 44) arranges financial assets according to liquidity and profitability. Liquidity measures the ease with which an asset can be converted into money and the certainty of what it will be worth when converted into money. Providing it is acceptable and can be used as a means of payment, money is the most liquid of all assets. However, in contrast to less liquid assets such as shares and government bonds (gilt-edged securities), money earns little or no interest.

Shares and gilts, which are generally more profitable than money, are also marketable — they can be sold second hand on the stock exchange. The stock exchange is part of the capital market on which public companies (plcs) sell new issues of shares to raise long-term capital, and on which the government sells new issues of gilts to finance its budget deficit (in fiscal policy).

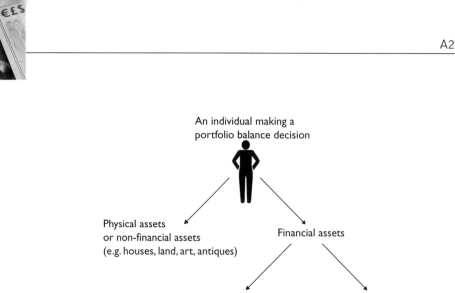

Figure 10 Different ways in which people can hold their wealth

Bank rate and monetary policy

Banks always need to hold a certain amount of cash to meet possible customer demand for cash. As a part of monetary policy, the Bank of England deliberately keeps the banks slightly short of cash, knowing that the banks will then have to get the cash needed to meet customers' demands from the Bank itself, by borrowing the cash at Bank rate. Until the introduction of quantitative easing, Bank rate was the key financial instrument through which monetary policy was implemented in the UK. It will again become the key instrument of monetary policy if and when quantitative easing is dropped as a monetary policy instrument.

Examination questions and skills

You should expect two main types of examination question on monetary policy. The first type mentions monetary policy explicitly, asking perhaps for an evaluation of its success, or for a comparison of monetary and fiscal policy. The second type of question is more general, requiring, for example, an evaluation of economic policy in stabilising the economic cycle. Monetary policy is not mentioned in the question, but a good answer would explain, analyse and evaluate how monetary policy (and also fiscal policy) might be used to control the level of aggregate demand in the economy. Monetary policy is a form of demand-side policy. Monetary policy is *not* a supply-side policy, though candidates sometimes wrongly argue that controlling the money supply is an example of supply-side policy.

Common examination errors

- Assuming that modern monetary policy is monetarist.
- Confusing monetary policy with fiscal policy.

- Confusing monetary policy instruments such as the interest rate with the policy objective of controlling inflation.
- Failing to realise that bank deposits are the main form of modern money.
- Failing to link interest rate policy to the central bank's lender of last resort function.
- Failing to understand that interest rate policy may become ineffective as inflation approaches zero.
- A lack of appreciation of the links between monetary policy and the exchange rate (see the final topic).

Fiscal policy, taxation and public expenditure

These notes, which relate to AQA specification section 3.4.2, prepare you to answer AQA examination questions on:
- the macroeconomic and microeconomic effects of fiscal policy
- interrelationships between fiscal policy and monetary policy
- the structure of taxation and public spending in the UK

Essential information

What you already know about fiscal policy, taxation and public expenditure
When studying AS Unit 2 you learnt that fiscal policy attempts to achieve the policy objectives set by the government using the **fiscal instruments** of **government spending**, **taxation** and the government's **budgetary position** (balanced budget, budget deficit or budget surplus). You also learnt that fiscal policy can be used as a demand-side policy or as a supply-side policy.

Demand-side fiscal policy
During the Keynesian era, fiscal policy was used primarily to manage the level of aggregate demand in the economy. When expanding or contracting aggregate demand, fiscal policy brings about a **multiplier effect**.

The government spending multiplier
As Figure 11 illustrates (page 46), an increase in government spending (or in any component of aggregate demand) causes multiple successive changes in national income, greater in total than the initial increase in government spending. This is the **multiplier**.

To explain the multiplier, Let us assume that there is demand-deficient unemployment, that the levels of taxation and imports are fixed, and that the government is initially balancing its budget (that is, $G = T$). To eliminate demand-deficient unemployment, the Keynesian government decides to run a budget deficit by spending an extra £10 billion on road building while keeping taxation unchanged.

- In the first stage of the multiplier process, income of £10 billion is received by building workers who, like everybody in the economy, spend 90p of every pound of income on consumption. It is therefore assumed that the **marginal propensity to consume (MPC)** is 0.9 throughout the economy.
- At the second stage of the multiplier process, £9 billion of the £10 billion income is spent on consumer goods and services, with the remaining £1 billion leaking into unspent savings.
- At the third stage, consumer goods sector employees spend £8.1 billion, or 0.9 of the £9 billion received at the second stage of income generation.

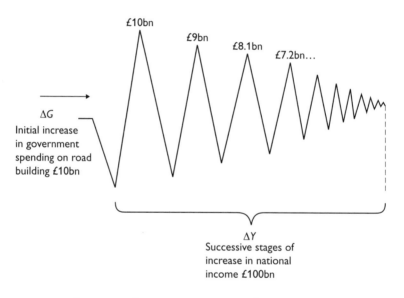

Figure 11 The government spending multiplier

Further stages of income generation then occur, with each successive stage being 0.9 of the previous stage. Each stage is smaller than the preceding stage to the extent that part of income leaks into savings. Assuming that nothing else changes in the time taken for the process to work through the economy, the eventual increase in income (ΔY) resulting from the initial injection of government spending is the sum of all the stages of income generation. ΔY is larger than ΔG, which triggered the initial growth in national income.

The decline and revival of demand-side fiscal policy

Fiscal policy is most powerful for managing aggregate demand when the multiplier is large (for example, 10 in the numerical example in Figure 11). In this situation, expansionary fiscal policy produces an increase in national income much larger than the increase in government spending or tax cut. However, in real life, demand-side fiscal policy is much less powerful. The size of the government spending multiplier is actually quite small (much closer to 1 than to 10) because, at each stage of the multiplier process, a large fraction of income leaks into imports and taxation as well as into savings, and is therefore not spent on consumption. Even more significantly, the multiplier process increases *nominal* national income, but not necessarily *real* national income. Over a generation ago, UK governments stopped using fiscal policy to manage aggregate demand because increasing the budget deficit simply injected larger and larger doses of inflation into the economy, irrespective of boom or recession. However, in 2008, there was a major policy reversal, though it remains to be seen (at the time of writing late in 2009) whether the return to demand-side fiscal policy will survive. The Labour government introduced a massive fiscal stimulus in an attempt to spend the economy out of recession. However, the Conservative Party, which was then in opposition, claimed that the main effect of larger budget deficits would be the public sector finances spiralling out of control.

Budget deficits, government borrowing and monetary policy

Budget deficits have to be financed by borrowing and this affects monetary policy in two rather different ways. On the one hand, the government can borrow short term from the banking system. When banks lend to the government, they create new bank deposits for the government to spend. Bank deposits are money, so this increases the money supply. Alternatively, the government can borrow long term by selling government bonds (gilts) to pension funds and insurance companies. To persuade these institutions to finance a growing budget deficit, the government may have to raise interest rates offered on gilts. But this raises interest rates in general, which discourages private sector investment in capital goods. This is called **crowding out**.

Do not confuse *financing* a budget deficit with using higher taxes or reduced public spending to *eliminate* a budget deficit. If the latter overshoots, a budget surplus results. Budget surpluses allow the government to repay past borrowings, i.e. to reduce the national debt (the historically accumulated *stock* of central government borrowing).

Supply-side fiscal policy

In the 1980s, supply-side fiscal policy replaced demand-side fiscal policy. Supply-side fiscal policy, which is microeconomic rather than macroeconomic, tries to alter incentives facing economic agents. Income tax cuts may make people work harder, while cuts in the real value of unemployment benefits (compared to disposable income in work) may encourage unskilled and low-paid workers to choose work rather than unemployment. Supply-side tax cuts may also encourage saving, investment and an entrepreneurial culture.

The UK government's fiscal rules

By creating conditions in which competitive markets function efficiently, supply-side fiscal policy aims instead to create macroeconomic stability. To try to achieve this outcome, in the late 1990s, the Labour government which had recently come into power announced a **Code for Fiscal Stability** in 1998, which based policy on two fiscal rules:

- **The golden rule** meant that over the whole economic cycle the government borrowed only to invest in new social capital such as roads and schools, and not to fund current spending, such as welfare benefits. The golden rule meant that the government was committed to balancing the budget over the economic cycle with regard to *current spending*, but not with regard to *capital spending*.
- **The sustainable investment rule** meant that public sector debt (mostly central government debt, i.e. the national debt) should be held at less than 40% of GDP over the economic cycle.

The Code for Fiscal Stability was a response to the fact that fiscal policy was no longer being used in a discretionary way to manage aggregate demand. However, a growing budget deficit also caused the government to increase stealth taxes, hoping that the general public would not notice. For electoral reasons, the government was unwilling to increase income tax to reduce the budget deficit, so it had to find other ways of raising revenue, such as by increasing National Insurance Contributions (NICs). However, in the 2008 Pre-Budget Report, the Labour government *suspended* (but did not *abandon*) the Code for Fiscal Stability. Perhaps the Code, or some fiscal equivalent, will reappear in some future year. The 2009 Pre-Budget Report stated that the Treasury plans to meet the golden rule in 2017–18, with the rule having not been met in every year between 2001–02 and 2017–18. (You must not confuse the Code for Fiscal Stability, which operated solely in the UK, with the European Union's **Stability and Growth Pact**.)

Automatic stabilisers

So far it has been assumed that the government must choose between demand-side and supply-side fiscal policy. This is not completely true. As the golden rule of borrowing indicated, the Labour government realised that, while fiscal policy should act predominantly on the supply side of the economy, there is a role for automatic stabilisers to influence aggregate demand in the economic cycle. Suppose the economy enters recession. As national income falls and unemployment rises, demand-led public spending on unemployment and welfare benefits also rises. However, if the income tax system is progressive (see below), the government's tax revenues fall faster than national income. In this way, increased public spending on transfers and declining tax revenues inject demand back into the economy, thereby stabilising and dampening the deflationary impact of the initial fall in aggregate demand, and reducing the overall size of the contractionary multiplier effect.

Automatic stabilisers also operate in the opposite direction to dampen the expansionary effects of an increase in aggregate demand. As incomes and employment increase, the take-up of 'means-tested' welfare benefits and unemployment pay falls automatically, while at the same time tax revenues rise faster than income. Demand is taken out of the economy and the size of the expansionary multiplier is reduced.

Direct and indirect taxation

Income tax is a direct tax because the person who receives and benefits from the income is liable to pay the tax. By contrast, most **expenditure taxes** are indirect taxes since the seller of the good, and not the purchaser who benefits from its consumption, is liable to pay the tax. Nevertheless, the purchaser *indirectly* pays some or all of the tax when the seller passes on the incidence of the tax through a price rise.

Progressive, regressive and proportionate taxation

In a **progressive tax system**, the proportion of a person's income paid in tax increases as income rises, while in a **regressive tax system**, the proportion paid in tax falls. A tax is proportionate if exactly the same proportion of income is paid in tax at all levels of income. Progressiveness can be defined for a single tax or for the tax system as a whole. For income tax to be progressive, the *marginal rate* at which the tax is levied must be higher than the *average rate* — though the average rate, which measures the proportion of income paid in tax, rises as income increases. Conversely, with a regressive income tax, the marginal rate of tax is less than the average rate, while the two are equal in the case of a proportionate tax. As a general rule, the average tax rate indicates the overall burden of the tax on the taxpayer, but the marginal rate may affect economic choice and decision making significantly, influencing incentives and the choice between work and leisure and decisions about how much labour to supply.

Progressive taxation cannot by itself redistribute income — a policy of **transfers** in the government's public expenditure programme is required for this. Progressive taxation used on its own merely reduces post-tax income differentials compared to pre-tax differentials. It is often assumed that the UK tax system is highly progressive, being used by governments to reduce inequalities in income and wealth. In fact, wealth taxation (or capital taxation) is almost non-existent in the UK, so inequalities in the distribution of wealth have hardly been affected by the tax system. Many people believe that direct taxes are strongly progressive in the UK, but this is untrue. Direct taxes, which for the most part are income taxes, are only slightly progressive for most income groups, becoming mildly regressive for the richest fifth of households. In 2010 the introduction of a 50% marginal tax rate on taxable income above £150,000 — a response to the deterioration in government finances — will marginally increase the progressivity of UK income tax. Because indirect taxes are mostly regressive, taking a declining proportion of the income of rich households, overall the UK tax system may even be slightly regressive.

Examination questions and skills

Along with monetary policy and supply-side policy, fiscal policy is one of the most important parts of the Unit 4 specification. Some examination questions obviously focus on fiscal policy as a policy *instrument*. Questions on policy *objectives*, such as growth, full employment and price stability, also require knowledge and understanding of fiscal policy and other policy instruments as the means to achieve these objectives.

Common examination errors

- Assuming that fiscal policy always means demand management.
- A lack of awareness of the supply-side elements of modern fiscal policy.
- Failing to understand interrelationships between fiscal policy and monetary policy.
- Defining progressive taxation incorrectly.
- Failing to appreciate the synoptic linkages between fiscal policy in Unit 4 and Unit 3 topics such as market failures and income distribution.

International trade, globalisation and the EU

These notes, which relate to AQA specification section 3.4.3, prepare you to answer AQA examination questions on:

- comparative advantage, and the case for and against international trade
- the pattern of international trade
- the impact of globalisation on the UK and world economies
- the European Union as a customs union and the Single European Market (SEM)

Essential information

What you already know about international trade

When studying AS Unit 1: Markets and Market Failure, you learnt that specialisation and the division of labour can increase production possibilities and economic welfare. In Unit 2: The National Economy, you learnt that an increase in exports shifts the aggregate demand curve to the right, but that an increase in imports has the opposite effect, taking demand out of the domestic economy.

Widening choice

A country which does not take part in international trade is called a **closed economy**. The goods and services which its inhabitants can consume is limited to those which its resource base allows it to produce. If the country is small, average costs of production are likely to be high because small population size and the absence of export markets mean that **economies of scale** and **long production runs** cannot be achieved.

A country which trades freely with other countries is called an **open economy**. Imports of raw materials and energy widen an open economy's production possibilities greatly, though in practice, open economies concentrate on producing the goods and services that they are good at producing, and import other goods and services. By exporting the goods they can produce competitively, open economies benefit from economies of scale and long production runs gained from access to the much larger world market. Likewise, imports lead to a vast array of choice and the possibility of a much higher level of economic welfare and living standards than are possible in a world without trade. To explain these benefits further, two important economic principles must be introduced: the **division of labour**, and **absolute and comparative advantage**.

Specialisation and the division of labour

When a worker specialises, he or she is employed to perform a narrow range of tasks, for example, teaching economics. Specialisation leads to a division of labour, in which different workers do different types of work. It also involves regional specialisation *within* a country, for example with the City of London specialising in producing financial services. Finally, there is international specialisation *between* countries, in which different countries specialise in different industries and then trade their surpluses. The international division of labour and successful specialisation reduces costs of production, and widens production and consumption possibilities.

Absolute advantage and comparative advantage

If a country is best at (or technically and productively efficient at) producing a good or service, it possesses an absolute advantage in the good's production. Absolute advantage must not be confused with the rather more subtle concept of comparative advantage.

To explain comparative advantage, let us pretend that the world economy comprises just two countries, Oceana and Eurasia, each with just two units of resource (for example, man-years of labour), which can produce only two commodities, guns and butter. Each unit of resource, or indeed a fraction of each unit (because it is assumed that resources or inputs are divisible), can be switched from one industry to another if so desired in each country. Finally, the production possibilities of one unit of resource are:

In Oceana:	6 guns	or	2 tons of butter
In Eurasia:	1 gun	or	4 tons of butter

In terms of technical efficiency, Oceana is 'best at' — or has an **absolute advantage** in — gun production, while Eurasia's absolute advantage lies in butter production. In this particular example, Oceana also has a **comparative advantage** in guns and Eurasia has a comparative advantage in butter. Comparative advantage is measured in terms of **opportunity cost**, or what a country gives up when it increases the output of an industry by one unit. The country that gives up *least* when increasing output of a commodity by one unit possesses the comparative advantage in that good. Ask yourself how many guns Oceana would have to stop producing or give up in order to increase its butter output by 1 ton. The answer is 3 guns, but Eurasia would only have to give up a quarter of a gun to produce an extra ton of butter. Similarly, the opportunity cost of one extra gun in Eurasia is four tons of butter sacrificed, but the opportunity cost of an extra gun in Oceana is only a third of a ton of butter. This tells us that Oceana has a comparative advantage in gun production and Eurasia has a comparative advantage in butter production.

Output gains from specialisation

Without specialisation, Oceana and Eurasia produce 7 guns and 6 tons of butter (assuming each country devotes one unit of resource to each industry). If each country specialises in the industry in which it has a comparative advantage, output changes to 12 guns and 8 tons of butter, that is, a *gain* of 5 guns and 2 tons of butter. (Even if it had been assumed that Oceana possessed an absolute advantage in producing both guns and butter, specialisation in accordance with the principle of comparative advantage could still lead to an output gain, though in this case the gain would result from *partial* rather than *complete* specialisation.)

Import controls or protectionism

Import controls can be divided into **quantity controls** such as **import quotas**, which put a maximum limit on imports, and **tariffs** (**import duties**) and their opposite **export subsidies**, which raise the price of imports or reduce the price of exports.

Supporters of free trade believe that import controls prevent countries from specialising in activities in which they have a comparative advantage and trading their surpluses. As a result, production takes place inefficiently, and the growth of economic welfare is reduced. But the case for free trade depends to a large extent on some of the assumptions underlying the principle of comparative advantage. Destroy these assumptions and the case for free trade is weakened. One assumption is **constant returns to scale**. In the example above, one unit of resource produces 6 guns or 2 tons of butter in Oceana whether it is the first unit of resource employed or the millionth unit. But in the real world, increasing returns to scale or decreasing returns to scale are both possible and indeed likely.

In a world of **increasing returns to scale**, the more a country specialises in a particular industry, the more efficient it becomes, thereby increasing its comparative advantage. On first sight, this increases the case for international specialisation and trade. However, increasing returns to scale can also justify import controls for developing countries attempting to promote the growth of new industries. This is the **infant industry** argument. According to this argument, new industries, which in poor countries have not as yet developed increasing returns to scale, need protecting from giant firms in developed countries, where increasing returns to scale have significantly reduced average costs of production. In the 1980s, the infant industry argument developed into a more sophisticated **strategic trade theory**, which argues that comparative and competitive advantage is often not 'natural' or 'God-given'. Rather, governments can create comparative advantage by nurturing strategically selected industries or economic sectors, typically those that make high-tech goods and use skilled labour. However, the selected sectors must be protected from international competition while they are being built up. The skills that are gained will then spill over to help other sectors in the economy.

When **decreasing returns to scale** occur, specialisation erodes efficiency and destroys any initial comparative advantage. A good example occurs in agriculture when over-specialisation results in monoculture, in which the growing of a single cash crop for export may lead to soil erosion, vulnerability to pests and falling agricultural yields in the future.

Over-specialisation may also cause a country to become particularly vulnerable to sudden changes in demand or to changes in the cost and availability of imported raw materials or energy. Changes in costs, and new inventions and technical progress, can eliminate a country's comparative advantage. The principle of comparative advantage implicitly assumes relatively stable demand and cost conditions. The greater the uncertainty about the future, the weaker is the case for complete specialisation. Indeed, if a country is self-sufficient in all important respects, it is effectively neutralised against the danger of importing recession and unemployment from the rest of the world if international demand collapses.

An argument opposite to the infant industry argument is sometimes made in advanced industrial economies to protect **sunset industries** in the older industrial regions from competition from new industries in developing countries. Keynesian economists have sometimes advocated the selective use of import controls as a potentially effective supply-side policy instrument to prevent unnecessary **deindustrialisation** and to allow orderly rather than disruptive structural change in the manufacturing base of the economy. They have also argued that it is better to employ labour inefficiently than for it to remain unemployed. Some economists also justify import controls to protect an economy from **dumping**, i.e. goods sold below cost to get rid of excess supply in the exporting country.

In addition, as demerit goods, such as narcotic drugs, and 'bads', such as pollution, clearly indicate, an *output* gain does not necessarily lead to a *welfare* gain. Governments believe that they have a moral duty to ban imports of heroin, cocaine and handguns, to protect the welfare of their citizens. Protection may also be necessary for military and strategic reasons to ensure that a country is relatively self-sufficient in vital foodstuffs, energy and raw materials in time of war.

The pattern of world trade

To many people living in industrial countries during the nineteenth century and the first half of the twentieth century, it must have seemed almost 'natural' that the earliest countries to industrialise, such as Britain, had done so because they possessed a comparative advantage in manufacturing. It probably seemed equally 'natural' that a pattern of world trade should have developed in which industrialised countries in what is now called the North exported manufactured goods in exchange for foodstuffs and raw materials produced by countries whose comparative advantage lay in the production of primary products — the countries of the South, or developing countries.

The actual pattern of world trade in recent years has changed from the nineteenth-century **North/South exchange** of manufactured goods for primary products. Most of the trade of the developed industrial economies is between themselves and with newly industrialised countries (NICs); only a relatively small amount is with the rest of the world. Much world trade is now **North/North**, i.e. high-income developed economies trading mostly with each other, though another important feature of modern world trade results from the shift of manufacturing industries to China and to other Asian economies.

Globalisation

Globalisation is the process integrating all or most of the world's economies and making countries increasingly dependent on each other. Globalisation's main features are:

- the growth of international trade and the reduction of trade barriers — a process encouraged by the World Trade Organization (WTO)
- greater international mobility of capital
- a significant increase in the power of international capitalism and multinational corporations (MNCs)
- a decrease in governmental power over MNCs

Free-market economists generally support globalisation, regarding it as inevitable and the major process through which economic development can occur in poor countries. Opponents argue that globalisation is a respectable name for the growing exploitation of the world's poor by international capitalism and American economic and cultural imperialism.

Critics of globalisation use the dependency theory of trade and development to argue that developing countries possess little capital because the system of world trade and payments has been organised by developed industrial economies to their own advantage. Export and import prices have, as a general rule, moved in favour of industrialised countries and against primary producers. This means that by exporting the same amount of goods and services to the South, a developed economy can import a greater quantity of raw materials or foodstuffs in exchange. From a developing country's point of view, it must export more in order to buy the same quantity of capital goods or energy, vital for development. (For further information about globalisation, see the answer to Essay Question 3 in the Questions and Answers section of this guide.)

The European Union as a customs union

The **European Union (EU)** started life in the 1950s as a **customs union**. At the time, Britain was not a member of the EU (which was then known as the European Economic Community (EEC)), preferring instead to belong to a **free-trade area**, which is another type of trading bloc. In a free-trade area, member countries abolish tariffs on mutual trade, but each partner determines its own import controls on trade with non-member countries. A customs union also creates intra-union free trade, but takes away members' freedom to set their own tariffs against non-member states. Instead, all members of the customs union impose a common external tariff on trade with non-members.

In 1993, with the creation of the Single European Market (SEM), the EU developed into a fuller common market. It did this by creating free internal trade in services as well as in goods, together with largely free mobility of capital and labour between EU member states. The **European Commission (EC)** is responsible for the smooth operation of the SEM. The EC is the EU's executive body, akin to the UK civil service, which implements EU economic policy to meet the requirements of EU political institutions such as the Council of Ministers. Currently, there are 27 Commissioners, each appointed by a different EU country and each with a specific responsibility such as agriculture or trade.

Examination questions and skills

Because the Unit title is The National and International Economy, at least one of the three essay questions in each examination is likely to be on international economics. Additionally, as their names indicate, the global context and EU context data-response questions inevitably have international dimensions, though these questions focus on the impact of one or more international issues on the UK macroeconomy. The four main topics to revise in the context of international trade are: the benefits and costs of international trade (particularly in relation to comparative advantage); the case for and against import controls; how the pattern of international trade has changed; and the impact of globalisation on the UK and world economies.

Common examination errors
- Writing descriptive accounts of the benefits of free trade devoid of theoretical underpinning analysis.
- Confusing comparative advantage with absolute advantage.
- Failing to appreciate the limitations of the principle of comparative advantage.
- Writing overlong and numerically inaccurate illustrations of comparative advantage.
- Assuming that free trade is advantageous for all countries, all of the time.
- Assuming that countries should always try to maximise exports and minimise imports.
- Asserting without sufficient evidence that globalisation is always good or bad.
- Wrongly describing the European Union as a free-trade area rather than as a customs union.

The balance of payments, exchange rates and the euro

These notes, which relate to AQA specification section 3.4.3, prepare you to answer AQA examination questions on:
- the difference between the current account and capital flows in the balance of payments
- how the exchange rate is determined in floating and fixed exchange rate systems
- the European Union's single currency and economic and monetary union (EMU)

Essential information

What you already know about the balance of payments, exchange rates and EMU

When studying AS Unit 2 you learnt very briefly about the current account of the balance of payments, and about how changes in interest rates (in monetary policy) and the exchange rate can affect the current account. However, Unit 2 did not cover capital flows, nor did it cover EMU and the euro.

The current and capital accounts of the balance of payments

The balance of payments measures all the currency flows into and out of an economy within a particular time period, usually a year. Until quite recently, the UK government divided the balance of payments into two main categories:
- the **current account**
- the **capital account**

To fit in with the IMF method of classification, **capital flows**, which comprised the old capital account, now form the **financial account** of the balance of payments, and the term 'capital account' is now used to categorise various transfers of income that were previously part of the current account before the new method of classification was adopted. Table 3 (page 57) shows the current method of classification for 2008.

The current account

The current account measures the flow of expenditure on goods and services, thus showing the country's income gained and lost from trade. The current account is usually regarded as the most important part of the balance of payments because it reflects the economy's international competitiveness and the extent to which a country is living within its means. Ignoring the other items in the current account, if receipts from exports are less than payments for imports, there is a current account deficit, whereas if receipts exceed payments there is a current account surplus. The current balance is largely determined by adding together the balance of trade in goods and the balance of trade in services. Trade in goods is sometimes called visible trade, and trade in services is called invisible trade. As Table 3 shows, the UK has a visible trade deficit and an invisible trade surplus. Particularly before the financial crisis that accompanied and partially caused recession in 2008, the earnings of

Table 3 Selected items from the UK balance of payments, 2008 (£m)

The current account *(mostly trade flows)*	
Balance of trade in goods	−92,877
Balance of trade in services	+54,479
Net income flows	+26,940
Net current transfers	−13,610
Balance of payments on the current account	**−25,068**
The capital account	
(transfers, which used to be in the current account)	**+3,393**
The financial account	
(capital flows, which used to be in the capital account)	
Net direct investment	−20,067
Net portfolio investment	+369,206
Other capital flows *(mostly short-term 'hot money' flows)*	−332,356
Drawings on reserves	+1,338
Financial account balance	**+18,121**
The balance *(errors and omissions)*	**+3,554**

Source: Balance of Payments, *Pink Book*, August 2009

financial services in the City of London have contributed significantly to the invisible trade surplus. In most years, the invisible surplus is insufficient to offset the visible deficit, so the current account is also in deficit.

The AQA specification does not require detailed understanding of all the items in the balance of payments account, but one other item in the current account needs explaining, namely **net income flows**. These provide an important link between the current account and capital flows. British residents (including UK-based multinational companies) invest in capital assets located in other countries. Investment in capital assets is a **capital flow** (see below), but income generated by overseas capital assets is part of the current account. Net income flows are the difference between these inward income flows to UK residents from capital assets owned overseas and outward profit flows to companies such as Toyota, generated by the assets they own in the UK.

Capital flows

Long-term direct capital flows occur when residents of one country invest in productive resources such as factories located abroad. Such investment can be either **direct investment** (explained in the paragraph above) or portfolio investment. **Portfolio investment** involves the purchase of financial assets rather than physical assets. Table 3 shows that in 2008, more long-term investment flowed into the UK than flowed out. Short-term investment, by contrast, was mainly in the opposite direction. Long-term capital flows are largely a response to comparative advantage, reflecting people's decisions to invest in economic activities and industries located in countries to which comparative advantage has moved. However, since changes in comparative advantage usually take place quite slowly, long-term capital flows tend to be relatively stable and predictable. The same is not true of short-term capital flows, which are largely speculative. These flows occur because the owners of funds believe that, by taking advantage of interest rate differences and by gambling on future changes in exchange rates, they can make a quick speculative profit or capital gain by moving funds out of one currency and into another.

Balance of payments equilibrium

Balance of payments equilibrium refers to the current account and not to the *whole* of the balance of payments. The current account is in equilibrium when export earnings and inward income flows more or less equal payments for imports and outward income flows. Disequilibrium occurs when there is a large deficit or surplus on current account. A large current account deficit may, however, be quite stable — providing it is financed by inward capital flows. As Table 3 shows, the net capital inflow of £18,121 million partially financed the current account deficit of £25,068 million.

Do not confuse balance of payments equilibrium with balance of payments *balance*. Like any balance sheet, the balance of payments must exactly balance in the sense that all the items included in the balance sheet must sum to zero. The final item in Table 3 explains this. The number in the balance (errors and omissions) item is simply the number required to make all the items in the table sum to zero. Note also the small size of the drawings on reserves item. This item shows that in 2008 the Bank of England bought pounds by selling reserves of foreign currencies. Central bank intervention in foreign exchange markets by selling or buying reserves is largely determined by whether the exchange rate is floating or fixed. Supporting a fixed exchange rate sometimes requires large-scale selling of reserves, but this is not the case with a freely floating exchange rate. Since 1992, the pound has floated freely; hence the relatively small size of changes in reserves.

Exchange rates

Exchange rates and a foreign exchange market exist because different countries use different currencies to pay for international trade. A currency's **exchange rate** is simply its external price, expressed in terms of another currency such as the US dollar, or gold, or indeed in terms of an artificial unit such as the **sterling index**, which is the weighted average of a sample of exchange rates of countries with which the UK trades.

Freely floating exchange rates

With freely floating (cleanly floating) exchange rates, the external value of a country's currency is determined on foreign exchange markets by the forces of demand and supply alone. Figure 12 illustrates how both the exchange rate and the current account of the balance of payments are determined in a freely floating system — subject to the very artificial assumption that there are no capital flows. If demand for pounds is D and supply is S_1, the equilibrium exchange rate, expressed against the US

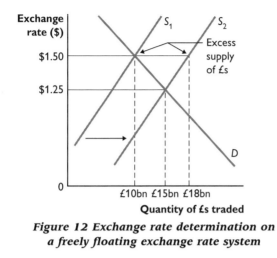

*Figure 12 Exchange rate determination on
a freely floating exchange rate system*

dollar, is $1.50. Assuming exports and imports are the only items in the current account of the balance of payments, the current account is also in equilibrium. The value of exports equalling the value of imports is £10 billion at the equilibrium exchange rate. When there are no capital flows, exchange rate equilibrium implies balance of payments equilibrium on the current account and vice versa.

Suppose that some event or shock disturbs this initial equilibrium — for example, an improvement in the quality of foreign-produced goods causing UK residents to increase their demand for imports at all existing sterling prices. Because the demand for foreign exchange to pay for imports increases, the supply curve of pounds shifts to the right from S_1 to S_2. At the exchange rate of $1.50, the current account is in deficit by £8 billion, which is also the excess supply of pounds on the foreign exchange market.

The market mechanism now swings into action to eliminate this excess supply, thereby restoring equilibrium, both for the exchange rate and the current account. The selling of pounds to get rid of excess supply causes the exchange rate to fall, which increases the price competitiveness of British exports and reduces that of imports. The adjustment process continues until a new equilibrium exchange rate is reached at $1.25 to the pound, with exports and imports both equalling £15 billion. Conversely, if the initial equilibrium were disturbed by an event that increased the demand for pounds, the exchange rate would rise to relieve the resulting excess demand for sterling, creating a new equilibrium at a higher exchange rate.

The advantages of floating exchange rates
- When the exchange rate is freely floating, current account surpluses and deficits cease to be a policy problem for governments and a constraint holding back the pursuit of the domestic economic objectives of full employment and growth. The

government simply allows market forces to look after the balance of payments, while it concentrates on domestic economic policy. And if, in the pursuit of the domestic objectives of full employment and growth, the inflation rate rises out of line with other countries, the exchange rate falls to restore competitiveness.

- With a floating exchange rate, monetary policy can be completely independent of external conditions and influences. There is no need to keep official reserves to support the exchange rate or to finance a payments deficit. The country's domestic money supply is unaffected by a change in official reserves, and interest rate policy is not determined by the need to protect the exchange rate. The country is free to pursue an independent monetary policy aimed at achieving purely domestic economic objectives, without the need to assign monetary policy and interest rates to support the exchange rate or to attract capital flows into the country to finance a current account deficit.

The disadvantages of freely floating exchange rates

- The argument that a freely floating exchange rate can never be overvalued or undervalued for very long depends crucially on the assumption that speculation and capital flows have no influence on exchange rates. This assumption is wrong. Most foreign exchange deals relate to capital flows and not trade, and exchange rates have become extremely vulnerable to speculative capital or hot money movements. A massive inward capital flow can overvalue an exchange rate and create a serious deficit on the current account.
- Floating exchange rates may unleash a vicious spiral of ever-faster inflation and exchange rate depreciation. Rising import prices caused by a falling exchange rate cause the domestic inflation rate to increase, which erodes the export competitiveness won by the initial depreciation of the exchange rate. A further fall in the exchange rate is then required to recover the lost advantage — and so on.

Fixed exchange rates

Figure 13 shows how a government and its central bank maintain a fixed exchange rate. Initially, the government fixes the exchange rate at a central peg of $2.00. Supply and demand determine the day-to-day exchange rate. Providing the exchange rate stays between a ceiling and a floor set when the fixed exchange rate was announced, there is no need for intervention by the central bank and the exchange rate is correctly valued for trade. However, Figure 13 also shows the exchange rate falling to the floor of $1.98, possibly because of a speculative capital flow against the currency. At this point the central bank intervenes, raising domestic interest rates to attract capital flows into the currency, and using reserves to support the fixed exchange rate. By selling reserves and buying its own currency, the central bank creates an artificial demand for its own currency.

Persistent support for the currency means that the exchange rate is overvalued, condemning the country to over-priced exports, under-priced imports and a current account deficit. **Devaluation** is a policy solution — in this case, a devaluation to a new central peg at $1.00. Alternatively, the government could abandon the fixed exchange rate and allow the currency to float downward and find its own level.

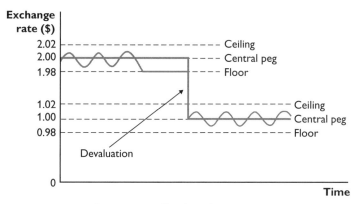

Figure 13 A fixed exchange rate

Although previously the pound's exchange was not fixed, late in 2008 and in 2009 the UK government seemed to encourage the exchange rate to fall in an attempt to bring about export-led growth which might drag the economy out of recession.

European monetary union (EMU) and the euro

EU countries currently divide into two groups. Most 'older' EU countries are in the **eurozone**, but the UK is among those choosing, at least for the time being, to remain outside the zone and to keep their national currencies. The eurozone countries are subject to a **common monetary policy** implemented by the **European Central Bank (ECB)** in Frankfurt. The pound's exchange rate floats against the euro, but some other non-eurozone currencies are more or less fixed against the euro.

Eurozone member countries can no longer implement independent monetary policies. In an important sense, national central banks such as the Bundesbank (in Germany) and the Bank of France are now branch banks of the European Central Bank which sets interest rates for the whole of the eurozone. This has led to the 'one size fits all problem'. Without the convergence of economic cycles in the different eurozone countries, each country might be in a different phase of its economic cycle, with some countries in recession or on the verge of recession, while others are in the recovery or boom phases of the economic cycle. Without convergence, a high interest rate is needed to dampen demand-pull inflationary pressures in fast-growing countries, while low interest rates are required to stimulate economic recovery or to ward off recession in other countries. The one size fits all problem stems from the fact that these requirements are mutually exclusive. In the outcome, the needs of core economies, particularly Germany and France, tend to override the requirements of periphery countries such as Ireland or Portugal.

Examination questions and skills

Examination questions are often set on the balance of payments and the exchange rate, and on the linkages between the two. A global context data-response question could test your knowledge and understanding of the causes (and/or the effects) of changes in the pound's exchange rate against the US dollar, or against a selection of world currencies. Similarly, a European Union context question could do the same with regard to the pound/euro exchange rate. The balance of payments and exchange rates are also likely to figure in one of the three essay questions.

Common examination errors

- Confusing the current account of the balance of payments with capital flows.
- Failing to appreciate the links between the current account and capital flows.
- Confusing current account equilibrium with balance on the balance of payments.
- Failing to understand how a floating exchange rate may eliminate a current account deficit.
- Writing one-sided polemical essays for or against EMU and the euro.

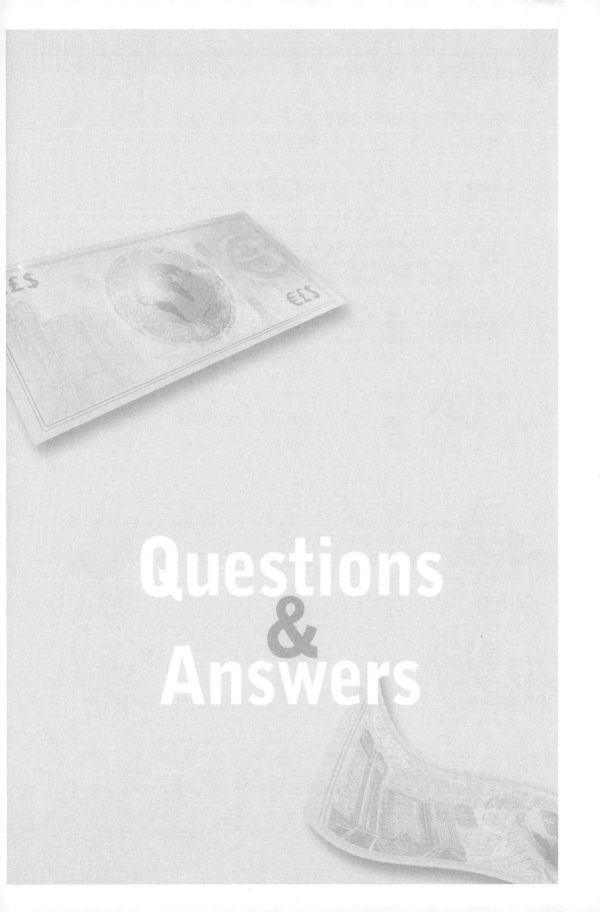

Questions
&
Answers

This section includes nine examination-style questions designed to be a key learning, revision and exam preparation resource. There are six data-response questions (DRQs) and three essay questions (EQs). The six DRQs are similar in layout, structure and style to the questions in Section A of the Unit 4 examination. Questions 1, 2 and 3 are set on **the global context**, and questions 4, 5 and 6 are set on **the European Union context**. For all the data-response questions, the word 'context' provides a scenario for analysing the impact of some event or events occurring in the wider world or in the European Union upon an aspect of the UK macroeconomy, for example, UK unemployment or inflation rates.

The three essay questions included in this book are similar to the three questions from which you must choose one in Section B of the Unit 4 examination. However, most if not all questions, be they data-response or essay questions, are likely to be of an *applied* nature, requiring application of knowledge and theory to analyse and evaluate real-world issues and problems.

This section also includes:

- A student's answer varying from grade A* to grade D standard for each DRQ and EQ.
- Examiner's comments on each student's answer, explaining — where relevant — how the answer could be improved and a higher grade or mark achieved. These comments are denoted by the symbol ℮.

Note: It is important to understand the difference between two types of marks that GCE examining boards award for candidates' work: **raw marks** and marks awarded according to the **Uniform Mark Scale (UMS)**.

Raw marks are the marks awarded out of 40 (for each DRQ and EQ) by the examiner who reads your script. After all the grade boundaries have been set as raw marks, each candidate's raw mark for the Unit 4 paper is converted into a UMS mark. UMS marks have the same grade boundaries — for all subjects and all unit exams. These are: grade A*: 90%; grade A: 80%; grade B: 70%; grade C: 60%; grade D: 50%; grade E: 40%. In economics, a raw mark of around 75% for both A2 Unit exams should achieve the UMS of 90% required for an A* grade, providing a sufficiently high AS mark has already been earned.

The marks awarded for students' answers to each DRQ and EQ in the following pages are raw marks, *not* UMS marks. A likely grade is indicated at the end of each student's answer, based on the qualities shown in each part of the answer. The following grade boundaries have been used: A*: 75%; A: 65%; B: 57%; C: 50%; and D: 43%. The boundary mark for grade E (which has not been used) is 36%. However, it must be stressed that the actual raw mark at which a particular grade boundary is set varies from examination to examination.

Data-response questions
The global context
Question 1 The impact of the global recession on the UK economy

Total for this question: 40 marks

Study **Extracts A, B** and **C**, and answer **all** parts of the question which follow.

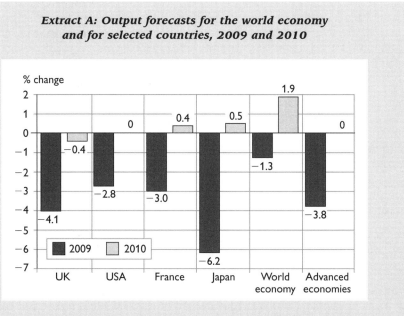

Extract A: Output forecasts for the world economy and for selected countries, 2009 and 2010

% change

	2009	2010
UK	−4.1	−0.4
USA	−2.8	0
France	−3.0	0.4
Japan	−6.2	0.5
World economy	−1.3	1.9
Advanced economies	−3.8	0

Source: IMF World Economic Outlook, April 2009

Extract B: The IMF's gloomy economic forecast

In April 2009, the IMF predicted that the UK would see its economy shrink by 4.1% in 2009, and by a further 0.4% in 2010. The IMF says this represents 'by far the deepest post-World War II recession', with an actual decline in output in countries making up 75% of the world economy.

data-response question

The IMF believed that only a recovery in emerging market countries would propel the world economy back into positive growth in 2010, albeit at a relatively weak rate of 1.9%. 5

Any recovery would be slower than in the past. There will be a smaller financial sector, with financing harder to come by than in the past, which will cramp economic growth. Rich countries such as the UK will face the burden of reducing their budget 10 deficits which have soared during the crisis, at a time when their ageing populations mean they will have lower tax revenues.

Source: news reports, 2009

Extract C: The 'decoupling' debate

Before the onset of the global recession in 2008, many economists believed that the 1 growing importance of emerging markets in countries such as China and India had 'decoupled' the economic cycles of countries such as the UK from the US economic cycle. As a result, they argued, recession or boom in the USA would no longer affect significantly the UK economy. 5

The counter-argument was that, through the process of globalisation, economies have become more intertwined through trade and finance. According to this view, other countries' economies have become more synchronized with the US cycle, not less.

So which view is right? The answer may lie in the middle. Recent economic history 10 clearly shows that the recession which started in the USA as a result of the sub-prime mortgage scandal spread quickly to other countries, including the UK, through its effects on the world's financial system, American demand for imports, shrinkage of US investment in the rest of the world, and above all, the collapse of consumer and business confidence. 15

Yet at the same time, recession hardly affected the Chinese and Indian economies. After a relatively slight downturn, economic growth in China and India quickly returned to annual rates of GDP growth of close to 10%. Have China and India become the saviours of older industrialised economies? And has rapid recovery in China and India tipped the balance of economic power away from the EU and North 20 America to south and south-east Asia?

Source: news reports, 2009

(1) Using Extract A, identify two points of comparison between the forecast changes in output for the two years 2009 and 2010. (5 marks)

(2) 'The IMF believed that only a recovery in emerging market countries would propel the world economy back into positive growth' (Extract B, lines 5–6). Explain the meaning of the term 'positive growth' and analyse how recovery in emerging market countries could propel the United Kingdom economy back into positive growth. (10 marks)

(3) Using the data and your economic knowledge, evaluate the view that UK economic performance is no longer highly dependent on how well the US economy is doing. (25 marks)

■ ■ ■

Candidate's answer

(1) The forecast changes in output were negative for all the countries and groups of countries shown in 2009, but positive in 2010 (with the exception of the UK where it was negative, and for the USA and all advanced economies where zero growth was forecast). For example, Japan was forecast to suffer a negative growth rate of 6.2% in 2009, and a positive growth rate of 0.5% in 2010. My second point of comparison is that with exception of the whole world economy, the negative growth rates in 2009 were significantly larger than the positive growth rates in 2010. For example in France, as an absolute number, i.e. ignoring the minus and plus signs, the negative growth rate of 3.0% in 2009 was nearly eight times larger than the 2010 positive growth rate of 0.4%.

5/5 marks

e Part (1) of the Unit 4 (and 3) data-response questions is no more difficult than the similar questions set in the Units 1 and 2 AS examinations. Given the wording of the question, all you have to do to earn full marks is to identify and briefly describe two points of comparison, and to back up each point with evidence provided by the statistics in the data. The candidate has done this, so earns all 5 marks. When she writes about absolute numbers, the candidate also displays a degree of statistical knowledge. However, this knowledge is not required for A-level economics, so full marks would still have been earned without its inclusion in the answer.

(2) Positive growth can be defined as an increase in the level of real output over a particular time period, for example, a year. It can also be defined as an increase in the potential output an economy can produce, associated with an outward movement of the economy's production possibility frontier. The term 'emerging market' is used to describe a newly industrialising (or industrialised) economy such as one of the so-called BRIC economies (Brazil, Russia, India and China). In the short run, though not necessarily in the long run, economic growth (or recovery from recession) is caused by an increase in aggregate demand. This can result from a positive change in any of the components of aggregate demand shown on the right-hand side of the aggregate demand equation:

$AD = C + I + G + (X = M)$

data-response question

$(X = M)$ is net export demand. If the UK's exports increase, while imports remain unchanged (or don't rise as much), export-led growth results. In the diagram below, the increase in net exports shifts the AD curve to the right, from AD_1 to AD_2. Output rises from y_1 to y_2, which means that short-run economic growth is taking place.

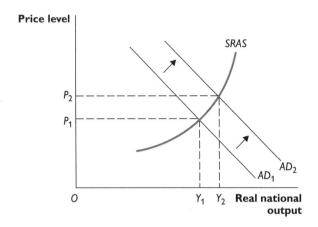

In the current world economy, the shift of regional economic power to emerging market economies means that demand for British goods triggered by the fact that they recovered earlier from the 2008 recession than the UK, has meant that UK firms did indeed have the potential to benefit from export-led growth.

10/10 marks

e This is an excellent answer that earns full marks. The candidate provides a good, clear definition, though to some extent she is mixing up the *measurement* of growth with the *definition* of growth. However, she is not penalised for this. Note how the candidate resists the temptation to evaluate the processes she describes. Part (2) questions are about explanation and analysis, and do not require evaluation. She introduces the distinction between short-run and long-run growth, but does not elaborate unnecessarily on the distinction. The question does not require a diagram (and full marks can thus be earned without the inclusion of a diagram), but the *AD/AS* diagram adds to the overall quality of the answer.

(3) UK economic performance relates to how well (or badly) the British economy has recently performed (and is currently performing) with regard to the standard objectives of government macroeconomic policy. These are: reducing unemployment, achieving economic growth and higher living standards, controlling inflation, and achieving a satisfactory balance of payments on current account (or possibly a desired exchange rate for the economy). Good performance means that employment is growing (and unemployment is falling), maintaining or even improving the economy's sustainable growth rate (and reducing fluctuations around the trend growth rate associated with the economic cycle), achieving a satisfactory rate of inflation, and maintaining or improving the international competitiveness of UK businesses. Bad performance means the opposite.

There is a saying frequently trotted out in newspapers: when the USA sneezes, the rest of the world catches a cold. This saying alludes to the fact that for several decades, the US economy has been the largest and most dominant in the world, a major market for other countries' exports, and a source of foreign direct investment (FDI) flows as US companies such as Ford and Microsoft invest in factories, supermarkets (e.g. Asda) and other businesses in countries such as Britain. When the American economy booms, the UK does well, benefiting from the demand from the huge American market for British exports, and the investment funds flowing from the USA to the UK. This induces export-led growth in the UK, and in terms of my earlier diagram (in my answer to part (2)), this causes the *AD* curve to shift to the right, which promotes economic growth and reduces unemployment in the UK. (However, as the diagram also shows, it may also lead to excess demand pulling up the price level, i.e. demand-pull inflation.) If this happens, UK national performance deteriorates, at least in the sense of maintaining control over inflation.

Just before recession hit the US economy in 2008, it became fashionable to ask: *have other countries 'decoupled' their economies from that of the USA?* If decoupling had taken place, recession and boom in America might not lead inevitably to recession and boom in the UK and in other countries. It was argued that the size and rate of growth of emerging markets in BRIC countries and other 'less developed' countries, might mean that they, rather than the USA, had emerged as the main markets and source of FDI for the UK economy.

In my view, the truth currently lies midway between the two extreme possibilities. There is plenty of evidence (Russians investing in English football clubs, the UK selling financial services to China) that the BRIC countries have become more important for the British economy and that they suffered less from the 2008 global recession. Yet by the opposite token, the recession (or at least the slowdown) suffered by virtually every country in the world in 2008 and 2009, emanated from the collapse in US demand and investment in other countries. This collapse was caused in large part by the 2007 'credit crunch', the US sub-prime mortgage problems, and the international financial crisis following the collapse of the US Lehman Brothers Bank in 2008. The rest of the world did indeed catch a cold as a result of crisis and recession in the USA. But recent events support the view that economic power is shifting from North America and west Europe to Asia. Asian countries are now much less willing to hold the US dollar in their currency reserves and to use the current account surpluses gained from exporting to the USA to supply America with a stream of savings to invest in the US economy. **24/25 marks**

data-response question

This is a rather discursive question that does not lend itself to straightforward application of the *AD/AS* model or to the use of production possibility curves and other diagrams to illustrate the points being made. However, in this case, the candidate has written an excellent answer that reaches the highest Level 5, which requires good analysis and also good evaluation. To reach Level 5 (and hence a mark between 22 and 25, with a midpoint at 24), a candidate has to display *most* but not all of the Level 5 qualities set out in the mark scheme.

At one point in the answer, to save having to repeat herself by drawing the same diagram twice, the candidate refers back to her answer to Part (2). From June 2010, this might not be a wise strategy. From then on, the different parts of each question will be electronically assessed and marked by different examiners. The examiner marking Part (3) of your answer will not have read your answer to Part (2). This means you should answer the sub-parts of each question (including the essay questions) without referring to what you have written in your answers to other parts of the question.

Scored 39/40   97.5% = high A* grade

d 2 ata-response question

Question 2   The impact of commodity price inflation

Total for this question: 40 marks

Study **Extracts A**, **B and C**, and then answer **all** parts of the question which follow.

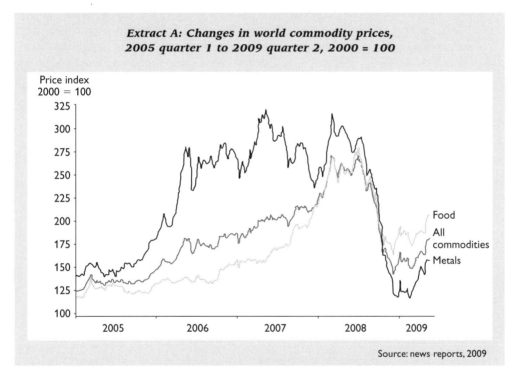

*Extract A: Changes in world commodity prices,
2005 quarter 1 to 2009 quarter 2, 2000 = 100*

Source: news reports, 2009

Extract B: Commodity price inflation

Why, in the recent world recession, were energy and commodity prices so high, and   1
in some cases, still rising? Shifts in demand and supply over the past several years,
provide much of the explanation.

Demand for energy and commodities has remained robust reflecting especially the
strong growth in emerging and developing economies, led by China and India. The 5
growth of these economies is more energy and commodity intensive than that of
more developed economies. In fact, emerging and developing economies as a group
have accounted for about 95% of the growth in demand for oil since 2003. The
prospect of a continued relatively strong expansion in these economies suggests that

data-response question

demand growth for energy and commodities will remain solid, even when global 10
growth is slowing or even becoming negative.

At the same time, the supply response to rising prices has been disappointing. In the case of food, agricultural production costs and associated transport costs are responding to rising oil prices. Temporary factors, such as droughts and bad harvests in some regions, have also played a role. 15

Policies in some emerging economies have played a role in increasing food prices. Recently, export restrictions, motivated by the desire to ensure that domestic populations have sufficient food, have been having negative effects on countries that rely on food imports, including some of the very poorest countries with highly vulnerable populations. In the case of rice, where the export market is small and 20 segmented, estimates suggest that export restrictions, and the resulting panic buying, explain about 50% of the increase in prices in 2007 and 2008. Such restrictions are also reducing incentives to increase production in exporting countries.

Amongst commodities, prices of metals tend to be the most sensitive to economic cycle fluctuations. Metal prices peaked in May 2007, then fell by 20% in the second 25 half of 2007, before rising again in the first half of 2008.

Source: news reports, 2009

Extract C: Commodity price inflation and UK inflation

In recent years, the policy response of the UK government and the Bank of England 1
to rising inflation has generally started from the assumption that inflation is caused by excess demand. Policy has focused on increasing interest rates (in monetary policy), to dampen the level of aggregate demand in the economy.

However, before recession hit the UK (and global) economy in 2008, which many 5 economists argued would lead to the problem of deflation replacing that of inflation, rising world commodity prices led to a severe bout of cost-push inflation. Because this cost inflation was imported from abroad, there was little the British authorities could do to stem the effects of rising commodity prices. In 2009, there was a danger that such cost-push inflation might be returning to haunt the British economy. 10

Source: news reports, 2009

(1) Using Extract A, identify two significant features of the changes in world commodity prices over the period shown by the data. (5 marks)

(2) 'Amongst commodities, prices of metals tend to be the most sensitive to economic cycle fluctuations' (Extract B, lines 24–25). Explain the meaning of the term 'economic cycle' and analyse why the prices of metals tend to be most sensitive to cyclical fluctuations. (10 marks)

(3) Do you agree that UK inflation can be controlled solely through the use of monetary policy? Justify your answer. (25 marks)

■ ■ ■

Candidate's answer

(1) The data in Extract A show a positive correlation (i.e. the values of the variables moving in the same direction) over the data period for all three measures of prices — for food, metals and all commodities. There were of course minor fluctuations up and down for each price measure, with metal prices fluctuating the most from month to month. Throughout the period from the first quarter of 2005 until near the end of 2007, the price index for metals (compared to the base year of 2000) was higher than that for all commodities, which in turn was higher than that for food. However the opposite was true for metals and food in late 2008 and early 2009. **3/5 marks**

> *e* The candidate clearly understands the data and obeys the instruction to identify two significant features of the data. In fact he identifies three, and possibly four features (correlation, short-run fluctuations, the ranking of the data series before late 2007, and the ranking from late 2008 onward). Despite the quality of the identifications, the candidate's mark is constrained to 3 because of his failure to select precise statistics from Extract A to support the points he is making. Part (1) questions usually ask for comparisons, but on occasion, as in this question, they ask for identification of 'features' in the data. Significant rather than trivial features must be identified, in each case backed up with evidence from the data. If the question asks for *two* features or points of comparison, and you write about more than two, the examiner awards marks only for the best two.

(2) The economic cycle, which is also known as the business cycle and the trade cycle, is the name given to the time path of actual real GDP over the course of a period which may last from about four to ten years. The main phases of the economic cycle, illustrated in my diagram below, are recovery, boom (in the upswing) and recession (in the downswing). Among the causes of economic cycles are fluctuations in aggregate demand and supply-side shocks throwing the economy off its long-run trend growth rate.

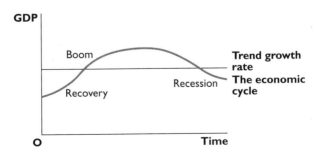

data-response question

The prices of metals are sensitive to fluctuations in the economic cycle, because of fluctuations in demand for metals in the different phases of the cycle. Metals such as copper are used in the building industry. When a lot of new houses are being built (because of growing business and consumer confidence) in the upswing of the cycle, the demand for copper increases, and with it the price of copper. Conversely, in the downswing, the demand for copper collapses, as does its price.

9/10 marks

> 🖉 For Part (2) of a context question, a maximum of 6 marks are available for explaining the term mentioned in the question, followed by a maximum of 8 marks for subsequent analysis. For full marks to be awarded, relevant explanation and analysis must both be in the answer. Two marks are usually awarded for a basic explanatory point, with further marks available for relevant development and diagrams. This answer earns 6 marks for evaluation and 3 marks for analysis. To earn more marks for analysis, a second argument is required, for example by drawing synoptically on the accelerator theory of investment learnt at AS level. (Remember, metals are examples of capital goods.)

(3) Inflation is a continuing and persistent increase in the average price level. Deflation is the opposite: a continuing or persistent fall in the average price level. The rate of inflation is measured by the annual changes in an index of average prices. There are two main price indices in the UK, the Consumer Prices Index (CPI) and the Retail Prices Index (RPI). These days it is the CPI that is used in monetary policy. Monetary policy can be defined as the part of government policy which aims to achieve one or more of the government's macroeconomic policy objectives using monetary instruments (mainly Bank rate, but also, recently, quantitative easing). Control of inflation is the main macroeconomic policy objective to which monetary policy is assigned, though when implementing policy, the Bank of England has also to take into account the general state of the economy (unemployment etc.).

Since 1997, the UK government has set the monetary policy objective or target, currently a 2% rate of inflation, measured by the CPI. It is then up to the Monetary Policy Committee (MPC) of the Bank of England to decide Bank rate, so as to try to achieve the 2% inflation rate target. The MPC has nine members, four being Bank employees, four independent economists appointed by the government, and finally the Bank's governor, who chairs the MPC's monthly meeting and using a casting vote if it is necessary. The committee members divide into 'hawks' and 'doves'. The hawks are generally in favour of increasing interest rates, while the doves want to reduce Bank rate.

The Bank of England believes that monetary policy affects inflation through a transmission mechanism shown in the following flow chart. Bank rate is shown at point 1 in the chart, eventually affecting inflation at point 11 at the other end of the chart. An increase in Bank rate increases other interest rates (point 2), such as mortgage rates, and also affects adversely people's expectations about the future course of the economy and the confidence with which these expectations are held (point 4). An increase in Bank rate should also reduce asset prices (point 3), such as the price of housing. Higher interest rates cause financial capital to flow into the pound, which causes the exchange rate to rise (point 5). This increases UK export prices, but reduces those of imports (point 10). Overseas demand for UK-produced goods falls.

Overall, following a Bank rate increase, aggregate demand (point 8) falls, as a result of the fall in domestic demand within the UK economy (point 6) and changes in exports and imports (point 7).

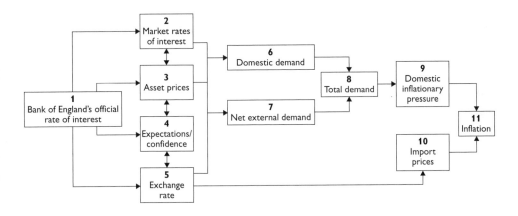

11/25 marks

Despite the candidate's obvious detailed knowledge of monetary policy, this answer disappoints. While it is always good to start an extended answer by defining key terms and concepts in the question, the candidate goes overboard in this respect. However, this is not the answer's major failing — the set question has not been answered. The candidate instead has written all he knows about monetary policy, while at the same time focusing far too much on the transmission mechanism through which changes in Bank rate affect aggregate demand and then inflation. Don't bother learning in any detail about the transmission mechanism. Stick to basics by understanding how changes in Bank rate affect other interest rates, which in turn affect aggregate demand. At this point, simple use of an *AD/AS* diagram would be in order. Also focus on the key word that the candidate completely ignores: *solely*. The answer contains good, but narrow analysis and absolutely no evaluation. The candidate's technical knowledge and analysis of the transmission mechanism of monetary policy might allow Level 3 (12 to 16 marks) to be reached. However, I have placed the answer at the top end of Level 2 (7 to 11 marks) because of the failure to address the set question and to refer, explicitly or implicitly, to the word 'solely'.

Scored 23/40   58% = low B grade

ata-response question

Question 3   Trade, protectionism and the UK economy

Total for this question: 40 marks

Study **Extracts A** and **B**, and then answer **all** parts of the question which follow.

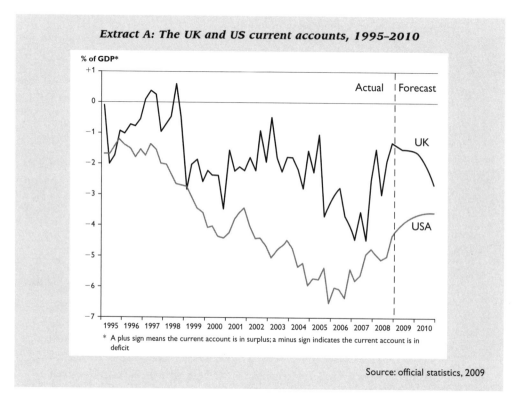

Extract A: The UK and US current accounts, 1995–2010

% of GDP*

Actual | Forecast

UK

USA

* A plus sign means the current account is in surplus; a minus sign indicates the current account is in deficit

Source: official statistics, 2009

Extract B: Recession and the protectionist threat

Early in 2009, with UK industrial production suffering a year-on-year fall of 11.4%, 1
some economists urged the UK government to subsidise struggling UK
manufacturing firms. There had been plenty of action in rescuing banks, but little
direct support to help manufacturing firms through the downturn.

But government subsidy for industry is, in essence, just another form of 5
protectionism. However, when there was a synchronised global collapse in demand,
it could perhaps be excused as a way of keeping otherwise viable companies and
skills alive until conditions recovered and they could begin operating normally again.

Yet as the recession which started in 2008 deepened, the danger grew of a growing deluge of beggar-thy-neighbour protectionist measures, which will end up destroying 10 all the hard-won gains of wider trade liberalisation.

We draw much of our fear of protectionism from experience in the 1930s when the USA raised import duties to record levels. Demand was by then already so subdued that the new tariffs may not in truth have had the devastating economic impact sometimes attributed to them. You can have as much in the way of import duties as 15 you like, but in circumstances where nobody is buying anything, they are unlikely to help your own industries very much.

Few would seriously suggest history is about to be played out in quite the same way this time. Hopefully, we've moved on a bit since then. Anything as crude as what happened in the 1930s would require the whole framework of the World Trade 20 Organization to break down, and this doesn't seem at all likely.

But today, protectionism takes subtler, less obtrusive forms — subsidy, soft loans, Buy American, British jobs for British workers, and so on. Yet there is a growing weight of it, and this doesn't bode at all well for a recovery in trade and economic activity.

Protectionism interferes with the process of creative destruction, which brutal though 25 it might be, is a core function of the economic cycle. Instead of out with the old and in with the new, zombie manufacturers, kept alive on a steady drip feed of state aid, take their place alongside the zombie banks.

Philosophically, the UK government doesn't like the idea of protectionist policies such as wage subsidies, but if everyone else is doing it, can they really afford to stay out 30 of the game? If it can be sold as a way of preserving skills, or perhaps helping people retrain, then perhaps there might be a way. In any case, manufacturing production and sales cannot keep collapsing at the present calamitous rate without some eventual and fairly dire consequences for employment.

The game on free trade seems to be up. It's hard to believe it will end up as bad as 35 the 1930s, but we are fast sliding into a more protectionist world. Still, it ill becomes Britain, which as an entrepôt nation has more to lose than most from the closing up of national borders, to introduce its forms of protectionism in response to state subsidy on the continent and Buy American policies in the USA.

Source: news reports, 2009

(1) **Using Extract A, identify two points of comparison between the UK and US balances of payment on current account over the period shown by the data.** (5 marks)

(2) **'Protectionism interferes with the process of creative destruction, which brutal though it might be, is a core function of the economic cycle' (Extract B, lines 25–26). Explain what is meant by the term 'protectionism' and analyse this statement.** (10 marks)

data-response question

(3) Using the data and your economic knowledge, evaluate the view that the UK economy can benefit more from free trade than from protectionism. (25 marks)

■ ■ ■

Candidate's answer

(1) The US current account was in deficit throughout the period from 1995 until 2010, though the data for 2009 and 2010 was forecast data. The UK current account was in deficit for almost all the period, but small surpluses were achieved in the middle of 1997 and 1998. At the beginning of the data period early in 1995 the US deficit (at about 1.75% of US GDP) was a larger proportion of GDP than the UK deficit, which stood at about 0.25% of UK GDP. **4/5 marks**

> *e* The candidate makes two points of comparison, but only the second point is backed up fully with evidence from the statistics. For this question, the mark scheme states that 3 marks can be given for a point of comparison backed up by evidence from the data, but only 1 mark if there is no data support. This means a total of 4 marks in this case. Evidence provided from the statistics should always be drawn upon in answers to the first part of a data-response question.

(2) Protection means import controls. It can take the form of quotas which place a maximum limit on imports, and tariffs and export subsidies. A tariff or import duty makes imports more expensive in the home market, compared to prices of domestically produced goods. Export subsidies by contrast, make the country's exports cheaper abroad, compared to the prices of overseas produced goods.

'Creative destruction' is a term used in the 1940s by the Austrian/American economist Joseph Schumpeter as a possible justification of very large firms, and indeed of monopoly. Schumpeter argued that monopoly power gave large firms the ability to become more efficient by investing out of current profit, then reducing prices and forcing rival firms out of business. Creative destruction allows new technologies, products and ways of producing products to replace old outdated methods and products. It is an element of improvements in dynamic efficiency. Schumpeter went on to argue that economic cycles (though he was analysing long cycles of about 60 years) also promote creative destruction. In the downturn of the cycle, weaker firms go to the wall in a deep recession and their assets are gobbled up and put to better use by the firms that survive the recession, fitter and leaner. By propping up and rescuing the weaker firms, protectionism prevents or slows down the process of creative destruction. Extract B uses the term 'zombie manufacturers'. This describes the firms that survive the recession that should have been allowed to die and disappear. In horror films, zombies are the 'walking dead', leaving their graves at night to haunt the living. **9/10 marks**

> *e* Although the candidate displays a wealth of knowledge and evidence of background reading, her answer does not quite earn full marks. Having gained

4 marks by explaining the meaning of protectionism in the first part of her answer, she needed to apply the concept in a more focused way in her analysis in the second part of her answer. However interesting it is, the description of a zombie should have been sacrificed to free space for more relevant economic knowledge.

(3) If in the distant past, the UK had remained a closed economy and refused to trade with other countries, the goods and services we now enjoy would be limited to those that could be produced solely from UK natural resources.

But in a world of completely free trade, in which domestically produced goods have to compete with those from other countries, imports enter the country priced at the ruling world price of P_W shown in the diagram below. This price is lower than the price that would exist (P_1) if imports were not allowed.

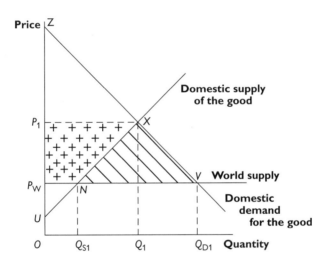

As a result of the fall in price, consumer surplus (a measure of consumer welfare) increases by the area bounded by the points $P_W VXP_1$. The area divides into two parts, shown on the diagram by the crossed and the striped areas. The crossed area shows a welfare transfer away from domestic firms to domestic consumers. The fall in the price from P_1 to P_W, brought about by lower import prices, means that part of the producer surplus domestic firms previously enjoyed now becomes consumer surplus. The consumers 'win' and the domestic producers 'lose'.

Consumers also enjoy a further increase in consumer surplus, brought about by receipt of the striped area. Indeed, the total increase in consumer surplus gain exceeds the size of the welfare transfer from producer surplus to consumer surplus. The country as a whole enjoys a net welfare gain, equal to the striped area in my diagram.

data-response question

The obvious logic of my argument is that if Britain uses tariffs to protect domestic UK industries, part or all of the welfare gain I have just explained will disappear, becoming in fact a welfare loss. Nevertheless various arguments can be used to justify import controls. Import controls, it is argued, can be used to protect infant industries while they grow. However, this justification is less appropriate for the UK than for a poor country trying to develop its industries from scratch. Rather, it might be more appropriate to argue that Britain should rightly try to protect sunset or geriatric industries (if there are any of them left) in older industrial regions from the competition of infant industries in countries in the poorer parts of the world.

19/25 marks

Although the candidate has used some very good analysis and has evaluated the arguments as she introduced them into her line of reasoning, I have placed the answer in Level 4 rather than Level 5. If she is personally justifying protectionism, the last sentence of her answer conflicts somewhat with the point she made about 'zombie' firms in her answer to part (2). However, this is not a significant criticism, and in any case from June 2010 onward, the different parts of the question may be marked by different examiners. The descriptor for Level 4 (17 to 21 marks) is 'good analysis but limited evaluation'. I have decided that the evaluation is too limited for Level 5 (good analysis and good evaluation), first because the answer ends a little bit up in the air, and second (and related to this point) there is no conclusion drawing arguments together. Nevertheless, taking all the answers together, the script just achieves an A* grade.

Scored 32/40   80% = low A* grade

The European Union context

Question 4   The impact of EU membership on UK macroeconomic performance

Total for this question: 40 marks

Study **Extracts A**, **B** and **C**, and answer **all** parts of the question which follows.

Extract A: UK trade with the EU and other groups of countries, exports and imports as percentages of UK totals, 1955 and 2008

UK trade with:	1955 Exports (%)	1955 Imports (%)	2008 Exports (%)	2008 Imports (%)
The European Union	15.0	12.6	56.2	52.4
Other west European countries	13.9	13.1	4.3	9.5
North America	12.0	19.5	15.7	9.4
Other developed countries	21.1	14.2	4.0	4.4
Oil-exporting developing countries	5.1	9.2	4.7	2.3
Other developing countries	32.9	31.4	15.1	22.0

Source: official statistics, 2009

Extract B: The European Union: a complete common market?

The European Union (EU) started life as a customs union in which goods could move 1
freely between EU member states, without tariffs having to be paid. In 1993, the
Union became a more or less full common market, in which services, labour and
capital could, in theory, also move freely between member states.

But these freedoms are not complete. Indecision and then the inability to impose 5
uniform standards relating to goods, and distortions created by member
governments favouring local suppliers, are two reasons why this is so. National

data-response question

governments still prevent foreign arms suppliers from competing in the supply of weapons, and the EU lacks a community-wide energy market. Competition is also discouraged in protected national energy markets from gas and electricity supply 10 companies located in other member countries. British energy companies, for example, cannot take over similar French companies, but UK utility companies have been acquired by the French. The French government even prevented acquisition of a yoghurt manufacturer, deeming the business to be strategically important for the French economy. In Spain, Bank Santander acquired Alliance and Leicester and the 15 Abbey bank, but British banks have found it difficult to take over Spanish banks.

Source: news commentary, 2009

Extract C: Macroeconomic performance in the UK and in the eurozone

Before 2004, the 15 countries then in the European Union were known as the EU-15. 1 These are the developed countries, sometimes known as 'old Europe', located in western Europe. Twelve of these countries have abandoned their national currencies, using instead the euro. The 12 countries within the EU-15 that adopted the euro became known as the eurozone. The UK is an EU-15 country, but is not in the 5 eurozone. From 2004 onward, the European Union admitted a further 12 countries, expanding the EU-15 to become the EU-27. New entrant countries such as Poland and Estonia, which make up 'new Europe', are mostly in central Europe. Other countries such as Croatia and Turkey may join the EU in future years.

Before 2008, the UK generally enjoyed a faster growth rate than the EU-15 and the 10 eurozone. Though unemployment fell in the continental EU-15 countries, the UK unemployment rate was lower than in countries such as Germany and France. From 1998 to 2008, the eurozone unemployment rate was significantly higher than the UK rate. Indeed, at the time, the UK was benefiting from the largest and the most long-lasting fall in unemployment in its recent history. 15

Inflation rates were also generally falling in these years, lying within the acceptable range set by the UK government in Britain, and by the European Central Bank (ECB) in the eurozone. Things changed of course during 2007 and in later years. After a sudden surge in 2007 and early in 2008, the rate of inflation fell, leading to fears that problems induced by deflation would replace those associated with a rising price 20 level. Unemployment began to grow in all EU countries as recession spread from the USA to Europe. With recovery from recession possibly beginning in 2009, growth is likely to remain depressingly weak and unemployment is likely to continue to grow, especially in the UK.

Source: news reports, 2009

(1) Using Extract A, identify two points of comparison between the UK's pattern of trade in 1955 and 2008. (5 marks)

(2) 'The European Union (EU) started life as a customs union in which goods could move freely between EU member states, without tariffs having to be paid.' (Extract B lines 1–2). Explain the meaning of the term 'customs union' and analyse possible benefits for a country joining a customs union. (10 marks)

(3) Using the data and your economic knowledge, evaluate the view that the UK's macroeconomic performance benefits from Britain belonging to the EU, but not having adopted the euro. (25 marks)

■ ■ ■

Candidate's answer

(1) Overall, with regard to both exports and imports as percentages of total UK trade, UK trade with the European Union grew, while trade with developing countries fell. Exports to EU countries grew from 15% of total UK exports in 1955 to 56.2% in 2008. By comparison, exports to all developing countries (oil-exporting plus other developing countries) fell from 38% of total UK exports in 1955 to 19.8% in 2008. Imports from EU countries grew from 12.6% of total UK imports in 1955 to 52.4% in 2008. Likewise by comparison, imports from all developing countries fell from 40.6% of total UK exports in 1955 to 24.3% in 2008. **5/5 marks**

✐ The question asks for two significant points of comparison. The candidate obeys this instruction and in each case provides sufficient evidence from the data to support each of the two comparative points. Full marks are therefore earned. Pleasingly, no attempt is made to drift away from the question, for example, by offering explanations of the points compared.

(2) A customs union is a group of countries that sign a multilateral agreement, not only to abolish tariffs or import duties within the union, but to impose a common external tariff on imports from countries outside the union. Along with a free-trade area, a customs union is a type of trading bloc. In a free-trade area, internal tariffs are also abolished, but each country is free to impose its own tariffs on imports from non-members, i.e. there is no common external tariff in the case of a free-trade area.

The main benefit of joining a customs union is to gain access to a larger market for the country's firms. The larger market results from tariff-free access to other countries' markets. The United Kingdom for example, with 60 million population, gains access to a market of over 300 million in the wider EU. This should enable domestic firms to enjoy much longer production runs and thus gain the benefits of economies of scale. Customs unions, along with other trading blocs, can be regarded as second best outcomes. The best, which is unattainable because not enough countries agree on its creation, would be free

data-response question

trade throughout the world. There would be no tariffs at all, and hence no customs unions. Given the impossibility of achieving this, a customs union creates a limited area of free trade. Free-market economists generally argue that a free-trade area is really the second best, and they relegate a customs union to third place position in the ranking of desirable outcomes.

10/10 marks

The explanation of the term 'customs union' earns all the available 6 marks. The rest of the answer is certainly good enough for the remaining 4 marks, displaying a succinct understanding of the nature of a customs union. If more marks and a longer time in which to answer the question were available, the candidate might have extended her answer by explaining that the benefits of a customs union depend on its size, whether it promotes internal trade in accordance with the principle of comparative advantage, and the extent to which it is trade-creating rather than simply trade-diverting.

(3) Macroeconomic performance is a measure of how well a country is doing in the world economy. Joining the European Union, but not having adopted the euro as the currency used in the United Kingdom, means that Britain can gain the benefits of the single market within the customs union, but still implement a monetary policy which is in the UK's national interest rather than one decided by the European Commission in Brussels and the European Central Bank in Frankfurt.

The countries now in the eurozone are no longer free to implement independent monetary policies. The European Central Bank sets interest rates for the whole of the eurozone. Prior to the creation of the euro, the EU attempted to achieve convergence in the economic cycles of the initial 12 member countries. Without convergence, each country would have been in a different phase of its economic cycle, with some countries in recession or on the verge of recession, while others were in the recovery or boom phases of the economic cycle. Complete convergence, by contrast, means that every country is in the same phase of the economic cycle. In the outcome, only partial convergence was achieved. This meant (before 2008 when almost all EU countries, including Britain, were hit by recession) that a high interest rate was needed to dampen demand-pull inflationary pressures in the then fast-growing countries such as Ireland, while low interest rates were required to stimulate economic recovery or to ward off recession in other countries such as Germany.

This led to the 'one size fits all' problem, which stems from the fact that these requirements are mutually exclusive. However, the political and economic power of Germany and France almost always overrode the requirements of countries on the periphery, such as Greece and Spain.

At the present time, the UK — though larger than Greece — is viewed in Brussels very much as a country on the periphery, semi-detached from mainstream

Europe. In the early 2000s, just like Ireland, the UK economy was booming. Higher interest rates implemented by a Bank of England separate from the ECB were therefore needed to prevent a bubble economy from emerging. If Britain had previously adopted the euro, it would not have been able to raise interest rates to pursue the country's national interest.

However, the argument I have just summarised may not be consistent with the evidence about what has actually happened. In the early 2000s, the ECB, far from behaving in an inflationary way, was in fact criticised for being too cautious and deflationary when setting interest rates for eurozone countries. By contrast, within Britain, the Bank of England's monetary policy ignored the rapid rise in house and share prices that was taking place. It wrongly believed that inflation was under control as an asset price bubble was gathering steam. When the asset price bubble was pricked, as was inevitable, the UK economy fell into recession before the eurozone countries also suffered an economic downturn.

In conclusion, therefore, I don't agree that UK macroeconomic performance has benefited from the country not having adopted the euro. However, being outside the eurozone does mean that the UK is free to devalue the pound's exchange rate in order to try to gain a competitive advantage for Britain's exports. Eurozone countries such as Spain and Italy can't devalue their currencies because their national currencies no longer exist. There may be some benefits from not having adopted the euro, but I think the costs of remaining outside the eurozone are greater.   **17/25 marks**

✍ If you refer back to the candidate's answer to Part (3) of Question 1 on pages 68 and 69, you will see how you should start the answer to a question which mentions economic performance, be it national economic performance or macroeconomic performance. This answer, by contrast, while mentioning macro-economic performance, says very little about what the term means. Consequently, the explanation does not really offer a platform on which to develop the answer.

But despite this rather woolly first sentence, *most* of the rest of the answer is good. The discussion about the benefits and costs of Britain adopting the euro is impressive. However, overall, the answer is lopsided because it provides only a very brief discussion, toward the beginning of the answer of the benefits (and costs) of EU membership (as distinct from euro adoption and membership of the eurozone). For this reason, I have decided to place the answer in low Level 4 (good analysis but limited evaluation), which covers the mark range 17 to 21. The candidate does make some good evaluative points, but as I have explained, the analysis is too narrow to justify a higher mark. Additionally, there is a rather limp conclusion.

Scored 32/40   80% = low A* grade

ata-response question

Question 5   Foreign direct investment, the UK and the EU

Total for this question: 40 marks

Study **Extracts A**, **B**, **C** and **D**, and then answer **all** parts of the question which follow.

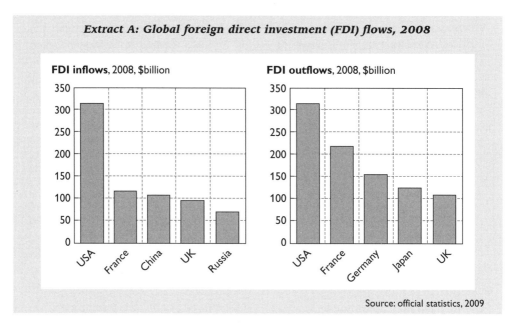

Extract A: Global foreign direct investment (FDI) flows, 2008

FDI inflows, 2008, $billion

FDI outflows, 2008, $billion

Source: official statistics, 2009

Extract B: What is foreign direct investment?

Foreign direct investment (FDI) involves the acquisition of real and useful productive 1
assets such as factories, oil refineries, offices and shopping malls in the countries into
which the investment is directed.

Outward investment occurs when British multinational companies set up subsidiary
companies from scratch in other countries or acquire, through merger or takeover, 5
overseas companies. An example of outward direct investment would be ICI
investing in a chemical factory in a developing country. Conversely, the decision by
the Japanese vehicle manufacturer Nissan to invest in an automobile factory in
Britain was an example of inward FDI. Arguably, direct capital flows into and out of
a country eventually lead to improvements in the balance of payments on current 10
account.

Source: academic research paper, 2009

Extract C: How EU member states compete for foreign direct investment

The creation of the Single European Market (SEM) in 1993 means that capital is generally free to flow without government restriction between EU member states. This has led to countries such as Germany and France establishing companies, factories, offices and shops in the UK, and UK firms such as Tesco doing much the same in other EU member states.

Some EU member states, notably France and Spain, try to protect their so-called 'national champion' companies from foreign takeover. But on the other hand, EU countries compete with each other to attract inward investment both from other EU member states and from non-member countries such as the USA, Japan and South Korea. In the 1990s, France accused Britain of encouraging artificially low wages, in order to attract French investment into the UK. France called this 'social dumping'. But British wage rates are still high in comparison to those paid in 'new' EU member states such as the Czech Republic and Hungary. As a result, FDI has been leaving the UK and other 'older' EU member states, moving east to central Europe. In 2009, the US computer company Dell decided to relocate its EU factories from Ireland to Poland.

Source: news reports, 2009

Extract D: Where does Britain stand in the FDI league table?

However you present the data, the fact remains that the UK has self-evidently become a less attractive haven for inward investment. There is no doubt that the UK has signalled to the world that it is not so interested in inward investment. We look like losing about 20% of the hedge funds to Switzerland, and a number of UK-registered companies, including the giant advertising company WPP, are moving their legal headquarters abroad. When such a company moves offshore, it advertises the fact that the UK has become a less attractive business location.

Recent falls in the pound's exchange rate against the euro may partially reverse this trend. But what should be of great worry is the growing trend for FDI to bypass the wider EU as well as the UK, moving instead to emerging market countries. South and east Asia benefit from huge direct investment inflows, while at the same time China is investing on a massive scale in Africa in order to control its access to raw materials.

Source: news reports, 2009

5

data-response question

(1) Using Extract A, identify two points of comparison between foreign direct investment (FDI) flows affecting the UK and other EU countries in 2008. (5 marks)

(2) Extract B (lines 9–11) states that foreign direct investment into and out of a country leads to an improvement in the balance of payments on current account. Explain the meaning of investment and analyse the relationship between direct capital flows and a country's balance of payments on current account. (10 marks)

(3) Evaluate the view that the UK government should ensure that UK savings are invested in UK industries, instead of relying on attracting foreign direct investment into the UK from other EU countries. (25 marks)

Candidate's answer

(1) Foreign direct investment (FDI) comprises investment in a country's companies made by overseas-based multinational companies. France and Germany are the only EU countries, other than the UK, shown in Extract A. In 2008, FDI inflows into France, at just over $100 billion, were greater than the inflows into the UK, which were just under $100 billion. For outflows, France again led the way. About $220 billion flowed out of France, compared to about $110 billion for the UK (and about $155 billion for Germany). As inflows into Germany are not shown in Extract A, they may be quite small, leading to the conclusion that Germany is a large net exporter of investment funds. **5/5 marks**

> This is an excellent answer that earns full marks. Strictly, the candidate did not need to define FDI in this answer, or to offer a possible explanation of Germany's FDI in the last part of her answer. The data in Extract A are actually quite limited, so not many relevant points of comparison could be made. Pleasingly, the candidate was not deflected into bringing the USA, China, Russia or Japan into her answer.

(2) Investment is the purchase of capital good by firms, both fixed capital goods such as machinery and variable capital goods such as stocks of raw materials. Foreign direct investment into the UK by companies such as Nissan (a Japanese car manufacturer) equips the UK economy with modern state-of-the-art factories. These produce high-quality goods that are in demand, not only in the UK, but in other countries too. This contributes to import-saving, because UK residents substitute British-made Nissan cars for imported cars. It also leads to exports of British-made cars, particularly to the other countries of the EU to which Britain enjoys tariff-free access. **7/10 marks**

> For a Part (2) question, 2 marks are available for a basic explanation of the term or concept in the question. For this question, the candidate writes an accurate single-sentence definition of investment with some development, and so earns 4 marks. A slightly woollier definition might also have earned 4 marks because

of the examples provided in the answer. Remember, it is always a good idea to provide an example or two. The second part of the answer is also succinct and accurate, but in this case earns only 3 more marks. This is because the answer ignores the effect on the UK current account resulting from outward investment by British firms into other countries. Firms invest overseas because they hope to make profits in future years. If successful, some or all of the profit will be repatriated to the UK as an investment income inflow in the current account of the UK balance of payments. Likewise, the profit made by Nissan from its British factory is likely to flow back to Japan as an investment income outflow. You should have learnt about this at AS.

(3) Saving and investment are not the same thing. Saving is simply the decision not to spend, whereas investment, as I explained in my previous answer, is the purchase by firms of capital goods. In a free-market economy, not subject to government interference, the self-interest of households and firms decides saving and investment decisions. Unless they hoard (for example by stuffing money under the mattress), households lend their savings to firms, either by purchasing new issues of company shares, or via the intermediary of financial institutions such as banks, insurance companies and pension funds. The flow of saving into investment is illustrated in the circular flow diagram below:

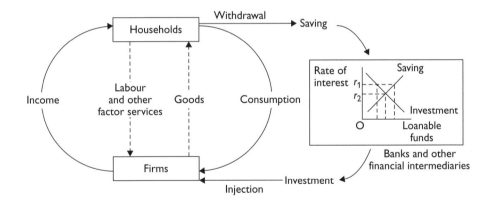

When lending to banks, households are likely to save more when the rate of interest is high. Conversely, firms invest more, and borrow more savings to finance their investments, when the rate of interest is low. In a free-market system, the rate of interest rises or falls to bring saving into line with investment. Intervention or encouragement by the government is simply not needed.

It follows that if the market mechanism and not the government should be relied upon to direct savings into productive investment, the question has been answered. The government should simply ignore foreign direct investment and leave everything to self-interest and to the market. **11/25 marks**

data-response question

This is a difficult answer to mark and grade. What the candidate writes is quite deep-seated and is well rooted in economic theory. The candidate shows also that she has learnt well and remembered the circular flow model of the economy, which is part of the AS specification.

When judging whether an answer fits into a particular level in the mark scheme for Part (3) answers, the examiner asks whether *most* of the criteria set out in the mark scheme have been met. For Level 3 a candidate must provide an adequate answer with some correct analysis but very limited evaluation. I have judged that this answer meets some, but too few, of the Level 3 criteria. The answer is much too narrow and does not discuss and analyse outward investment from the UK to other EU countries, or inward investment from continental Europe into the UK. Absolutely no knowledge is shown of the EU as a customs union, the single market and the free movement of capital and labour within the European Union. In a European Union context answer, at least some mention must be made of these to reach Level 3. Narrowness of content in the answer means that there really isn't any relevant evaluation. Hence I have decided to award a high Level 2 mark, and even this may be generous.

Scored 23/40 58% = low B grade

Question 6 Fiscal policy and government borrowing in the UK and the EU

Total for this question: 40 marks

Study **Extracts A**, **B and C**, and then answer **all** parts of the question which follow.

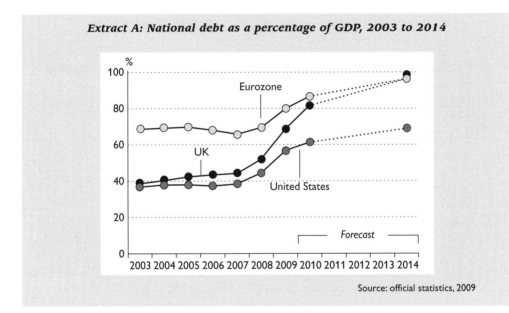

Extract A: National debt as a percentage of GDP, 2003 to 2014

Source: official statistics, 2009

Extract B: Government borrowing and debt, in the UK and the EU

The European Union's Stability and Growth Pact (SGP) requires that *all* EU member 1
countries agree to limit their budget deficits as a proportion of GDP. In normal times
all members of the European Union (and not only the eurozone members) are meant
to aim for balanced budgets, or small budget deficits or surpluses. Governments that
run fiscal deficits bigger than 3% of GDP must take swift corrective action. If a 5
eurozone country breaks the 3% limit for more than 3 years in a row, it becomes
liable to fines of billions of euros. These provisions are meant to be so intimidating
that no government dares breach the 3% rule, but in practice, it has not worked out
like that.

6

data-response question

Governments have to borrow to finance a budget deficit, and government borrowing 10
adds to government debt (the national debt). By the end of 2009 UK government
borrowing was growing at a much faster rate than borrowing in other EU countries.
This is likely to pose huge problems for the UK economy in future years. Action must
therefore be taken to reduce the size of UK government borrowing, not so much to
meet the Stability and Growth Pact's rules, but to save the British economy.   15

Source: academic research paper, 2009

Extract C: Should the fiscal stimulus be ended?

The Chancellor of the Exchequer has warned that the world could be dragged into a 1
double-dip recession if other governments stop using an expansionary fiscal policy to
stimulate their economies. He said he would oppose moves by France and Germany
to end the fiscal stimulus policies they had cautiously adopted to try to spend their
economies out of recession.   5

Britain's recovery from recession is lagging behind France and Germany, who both
returned to economic growth in mid-2009. Germany's Angela Merkel and French
President Nicolas Sarkozy are now keen to end the multibillion euro fiscal stimulus
packages that are credited with easing some of the pain of the recession, but which
have also sent government borrowing soaring. The UK Chancellor, though, is 10
determined to fight those who believe the crisis is over. In the last year the
government cut VAT, at least until January 2010, pumped billions into failing banks,
and authorised the Bank of England to engage in a quantitative easing programme to
try to restore normal banking conditions. Economists now believe that the cost in UK
government borrowing for this year alone will exceed Darling's target of £175bn.   15

The UK Chancellor's views are echoed by some of his counterparts around the globe.
Yesterday Jean-Claude Juncker, the chairman of eurozone finance ministers, said that
'while the worst is over for the time being, governments should be wary of
withdrawing fiscal stimulus measures too quickly'.

Source: news reports, 2009

(1) Using Extract A, identify two points of comparison between Britain's
national debt and eurozone national debt over the period shown by the
data.   (5 marks)

(2) 'Governments have to borrow to finance a budget deficit, and government
borrowing adds to government debt' (Extract B, lines 10–11). Explain the
meaning of the term 'budget deficit' and analyse the relationship between
government borrowing and government debt.   (10 marks)

(3) Extract C, lines 7–9, states that France and Germany were likely to end their fiscal stimulus policies, aimed to get their economies out of the recession, before the UK took similar action. Using the data and your economic knowledge, discuss whether the UK's fiscal policy should always be different from the fiscal policies of members of the eurozone. (25 marks)

■ ■ ■

Candidate's answer

(1) Britain's national debt level was higher than US national debt throughout the period from 2003 to 2014, except at the beginning of 2003 when they were about equal. Second, the debt level in all three areas rose at the same steady rate from 2010 onward, whereas debt levels varied from year to year before that. **0/5 marks**

> *e* This answer is bad on a number of accounts and earns no marks. First, the candidate has not read the question properly. For the most part he compares Britain's national debt with that of the USA, not with the European Union as instructed. Second, and possibly also related to hurried reading of the question, he interprets percentages of GDP with absolute national debt levels. As I am sure you learnt at AS, you must read the titles of the extracts and the labelling on the axes carefully so that you don't make this kind of mistake. Third, no statistical evidence is quoted from the data source to back up the points made. And fourth, the candidate makes a naive comment when comparing the forecast data with the recorded data for past years at the time the graph was drawn. The forecast data show the expected *change* over the whole period from 2010 to 2014, not the expected *data* for each year in the forecast period.

(2) A budget deficit occurs when the total value of imports exceeds that of exports. Government borrowing takes the form of selling National Savings certificates and premium bonds to people like you and me. We buy them because we think they are safe, but you can usually get a better deal from a building society such as the Nationwide. Government debt is the same as government borrowing; there is no other relationship between the two. **0/10 marks**

> *e* Again this answer earns no marks. The answer starts with a common error made by exam candidates: confusing the government's budgetary position (relating *G* to *T*) with the country's current account position on the balance of payments (represented by *X* and *M*). If you make this mistake in an exam and write about the wrong sort of deficit, you won't earn any marks. However, even when it eventually focuses on government finances, the rest of the answer is no better. A correct answer would focus on government borrowing as the flow of borrowing per time period (e.g. a year) required to finance the government's budget deficit (*G* > *T*). The flow of new borrowing, assuming that borrowing is not paid back during the course of the year, adds to the stock of government debt. The stock of central government debt is called the national debt.

data-response question

(3) Fiscal policy can be defined as the use by the government of the fiscal policy instruments, government spending and taxation, to try to achieve government policy objectives such as full employment, economic growth and control of inflation.

In 2008 and 2009 continental EU countries such as Germany and France (as well as the UK) were in recession. There was a lack of aggregate demand, and unemployment grew to approach 3 million in the UK by the end of 2009. (Some economists said that the true figure was much larger, possibly as high as 5 million as lots of the unemployed were not registered on the claimant count and the total number was underestimated by the Labour Force Survey.) Because there was general agreement that most of the unemployment was cyclical, resulting from deficient aggregate demand, many economists, particularly Keynesians, argued that governments and central banks should undertake a massive expansion of aggregate demand. They believed that if this did not happen, the already-severe recession would become a full-blown depression that could even be worse than the Great Depression of the 1930s.

Two main types of policy were called for. These were quantitative easing and very low interest rates (in monetary policy) and a huge fiscal stimulus (in fiscal policy). Quantitative easing increases the money supply. It was hoped that when people spend this money in a stagnant economy, aggregate demand increases and shifts the economy from point X to point Z in my production possibility diagram.

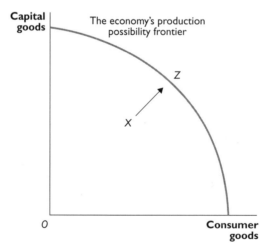

According to Keynesian economists, the monetary policy of quantitative easing and low interest rates should work in tandem with the fiscal stimulus brought about by tax cuts and massive increases in government spending. Again, it was hoped that the fiscal stimulus would help to shift the economy towards full employment at point Z on my diagram.

At the beginning of the recession in 2008, there was considerable agreement among eurozone member countries, and also in the UK, that such 'panic' policies should be undertaken. However, this consensus soon broke down. Germany and France decided that a massive fiscal stimulus was not required, possibly because their recessions were shallower and they were already beginning to see 'green shoots' of recovery, while the UK economy continued to languish. Even in Britain, leading Conservative politicians David Cameron and George Osborne broke ranks with the Labour Government and said that taxes should be raised and not cut, and government spending cut and not raised, in order to get the public finances out of the giant hole into which they were slipping.   **16/25 marks**

This is much better than the candidate's answers to the earlier parts of the question, reaching the top of Level 3 (an adequate answer with some correct analysis but very limited evaluation). This enables the candidate to scrape a grade D overall for the question. Nevertheless, because the answer is rather limited, it does not reach Level 4. Despite the instruction in the question, the candidate makes no explicit reference to the data. The mention of Germany's Angela Merkel and French President Nicolas Sarkozy in relation to fiscal stimulus policies in Extract C provides an obvious reference point. A Level 4 or 5 answer might also discuss the implications of the EU's Stability and Growth Pact (described in Extract B), explaining how the Pact supposedly limits the freedom of eurozone countries to set their own fiscal policies, while the UK, being outside the eurozone, enjoys more freedom.

Scored 16/40   40% = D/E grade boundary

Essay questions

Question 1   Inflation and deflation

(1) Explain different possible causes of inflation. (15 marks)

(2) 'Since the costs of inflation exceed the benefits of inflation, deflation must be good for the economy.' To what extent do you agree with this view? Justify your answer. (25 marks)

■ ■ ■

Candidate's answer

(1) Inflation is defined as a continuing or persistent rise in the average price level, or a continuing fall in the value of money. For example, when the annual inflation rate is 3%, goods which cost 103 pence today would have cost one pound a year ago. The rate of inflation is measured by the annual rate of change in the Retail Prices Index (RPI), or these days as far as the Bank of England is concerned, the annual rate of change in the Consumer Prices Index (CPI). The Bank of England currently implements monetary policy to try to achieve the 2% inflation rate target, measured by the CPI, set by the government.

There are two main causes of inflation, excess demand and rising production costs. The former is known as demand-pull inflation and the latter as cost-push inflation. Both are illustrated in the diagrams below (page 97).

In the left-hand diagram, one of the components of aggregate demand ($C + I + G + (X - M)$) has increased, for example consumption spending (C). This causes the aggregate demand curve to shift to the right, from AD_1 to AD_2. I am assuming that the economy is producing on its vertical long-run aggregate supply curve labelled *LRAS*. This means there is no spare capacity in the economy. Given this situation, the increase in aggregate demand creates excess demand. Consumers are spending more, but real output cannot increase in the short run. With output remaining at its full-employment level (y_{FE}), something has to give. The thing that gives is the price level, which is pulled up by excess demand. Macroeconomic equilibrium moves from point X on the diagram to point Z.

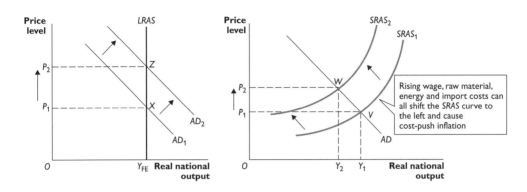

As the right-hand panel of my diagram indicates, cost inflation, by contrast, is caused by an increase in one or more of the factors shown in the 'box' on the diagram, wage costs, raw material costs, energy costs (especially oil costs) and import costs. When any of these increase, then assuming the cost increase is not offset by a cost decline originating elsewhere in the economy, the short-run *AS* curve shifts upwards and to the left, from $SRAS_1$ to $SRAS_2$. Macroeconomic equilibrium moves from point *V* on the diagram to point *W*. **11/15 marks**

e While it is always best to start Part (1) of an essay question by defining key concepts in the wording of the question, this candidate then does what many candidates often do when answering questions on inflation. In his first paragraph he just writes what he knows on inflation, including material that is not relevant for answering the set question. Fortunately, the drift is not too great, and focus is restored in the second paragraph.

This question could very well have been set at AS rather than at A2. At AS, this answer would have been quite sufficient to earn full marks. However, at A2 more depth of analysis is required. The candidate might have brought in the monetarist explanation of inflation and the role of the money supply when explaining demand-pull inflation. He might also have explained how the government's budget deficit and public sector expenditure can create excess demand for output. Likewise, he should have developed his explanation of cost-push inflation, for example, by explaining that when wages increase at a faster rate than labour productivity, not only might excess demand result, but employers' real costs of production increase. Faced with increased real production costs, firms that enjoy a degree of monopoly power raise their prices so as to maintain their profit margins.

(2) Inflation is generally considered bad for an economy because it distorts normal economic behaviour. When prices are constantly changing, consumers are likely to be confused by inflationary noise. Basically, this means that the signalling, incentive and rationing functions of prices do not work properly because the price changes associated with inflation send out confusing information. As a result, resource misallocation within the economy occurs.

essay question

If inflation is generally bad, is deflation therefore good? The answer is generally yes, providing people can maintain their money incomes. If money incomes remain the same, or even grow, then people inevitably become better off in real terms when average prices fall. Since one of the most important objectives of a government's macroeconomic policy is to raise real incomes in order to improve living standards, it follows that falling prices must be good.

12/25 marks

@ Although the candidate introduces and explains two good arguments into his answer, that is all he does. A wider range of arguments need to be considered, for example drawing on the benefits of inflation, as well as other costs, that are summarised on pages 34–35 in the Content Guidance section of this book. Much more needs to be said about deflation. The standard case against deflation is that it is associated with recession and a depressed economy. There is a danger that an excessive reduction in aggregate demand designed to bleed inflation out of the economic system will do more harm than good to the economy. According to this line of reasoning, it is better to live with low but stable inflation, as the necessary spin-off of a growing economy accompanied by consumer and business optimism. The flip side to this argument is that an apparently acceptable rate of inflation can quickly mutate into a high, accelerating and damaging inflation rate which is beyond the control of the government and central bank, except at the cost of accepting a massive recession and high unemployment.

Be that as it may, there are a number of other arguments the candidate might have considered. He could have debated the possibility that falling prices create incentives for people to postpone spending decisions, thus exacerbating deficient aggregate demand. Perhaps the most deep-seated approach would be to distinguish between a 'good' deflation and a 'bad' deflation. In a 'bad' deflation, average prices fall as a result of recession and a collapse of aggregate demand. By contrast, a 'good' deflation is brought about by increases in productivity and productive efficiency that result, in part, from technical progress. Falling real production costs throughout the economy cause the *LRAS* curve to shift to the right and the average price level to fall.

Perhaps harshly, I have decided to place this answer at the bottom of Level 3 (an adequate answer with some correct analysis but very limited evaluation). Apart from writing too narrow an answer, the candidate has insufficiently debated the issue posed by the question, namely, given the assumption that the costs of inflation exceed the benefits, can it be concluded that deflation is good for the economy? With this type of question, it is wise not to agree wholeheartedly, or by the opposite token to completely reject, the question's central assertion. Instead, it is best to adopt an 'it all depends' or an 'on the one hand this, on the other hand that' approach, also known as 'sitting on the fence'. However, if you adopt this strategy, to earn a high mark you must use evidence to justify your conclusion.

Scored 23/40   57.5% = B/C grade boundary

Question 2   Supply-side macroeconomic policy

(1) Explain how supply-side economic policies can be used to improve productivity, efficiency and national economic performance.   (15 marks)

(2) Assess the view that supply-side policies should be regarded as more important than demand-side policies in the macroeconomic management of the UK economy.   (25 marks)

■ ■ ■

Candidate's answer

(1)   Supply-side policies are the set of government policies that aim to increase labour productivity and to make markets function more efficiently and competitively. Supply-side policies thus aim to increase the economy's ability to produce within the country the goods and services that people want, and also goods that are in demand in export markets. Labour productivity is output per worker, and national economic performance is measured by the extent to which economic growth is achieved, jobs are created, inflation is controlled, and the country's industries are competitive in world markets.

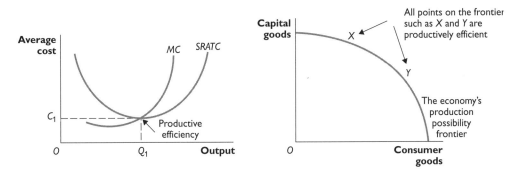

There are a number of different types of economic efficiency. Two of the most important are productive efficiency and allocative efficiency. Productive efficiency occurs when average costs of production are reduced to the minimum possible. The productively efficient level of output for a firm is shown in the left-hand diagram and for the whole economy in the right-hand diagram.

Allocative efficiency requires that resource misallocation is got rid of, or at least minimised. It requires the signalling and incentive functions of prices to function well in order to create the conditions in which scarce resources can be allocated between competing uses in ways which improve economic welfare throughout society.

essay question

At the macroeconomic level, perhaps the main supply-side policies are those that aim to increase personal incentives in labour markets. Supply-side economists believe that high rates of income tax and the overall burden of taxes upon taxpayers create disincentives in the labour market. The disincentives destroy the will to work, which, by reducing national income as taxation increases, then reduces the government's total tax revenue.

If the government wishes to increase total tax revenue, it must cut tax rates rather than increase them. A reduction in tax rates creates the incentives needed to stimulate economic growth. Faster growth means that total tax revenue increases despite the fact that tax rates are lower. Arguably the effect is reinforced by a decline in tax evasion and avoidance, as the incentive to engage in these activities reduces at lower marginal tax rates.
10/15 marks

e As I have mentioned in the context of earlier questions, it is always a good idea to define key concepts in the question. However, this candidate spends too long on definitions, given that only 3 or possibly 4 marks are available for explaining the meaning of key terms. The candidate should have devoted more of her answer to addressing the issue posed by the question, namely how may supply-side policies improve productivity, efficiency and national economic performance. While the answer links supply-side fiscal policy to national economic performance, there is no explanation of how supply-side policies might improve productivity and efficiency.

(2) Whereas demand management policies are essentially short term, supply-side policies try to improve the economy's ability to produce in the medium and long term, perhaps many years in the future. Supply-side policies, which are often microeconomic rather than macroeconomic, aim to increase the efficiency and competitiveness of all the markets in the economy: goods markets (or product markets), the labour market and financial markets. The expression 'first the pain, and then the gain' captures a key element of supply-side policy. By making it easier for firms to hire and fire workers, and by removing state support for industry, supply-side policies initially increase personal risk and insecurity. However, by creating incentives to be entrepreneurial, to supply labour, to save and to invest, supply-side policies may eventually improve long-run economic performance. Successful supply-side policies increase the economy's trend rate of growth, illustrated in my diagram below through the *LRAS* curve shifting to the right from $LRAS_1$ to $LRAS_2$.

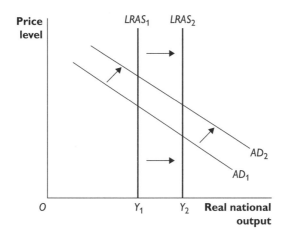

However, my diagram also shows the aggregate demand curve shifting to the right from AD_1 to AD_2. This illustrates the last argument I wish to make, namely that the role of aggregate demand should not be ignored when advocating the case for supply-side policies. Because supply-side policies increase the total level of output that the economy can produce, successful supply-side policies mean that aggregate demand must also increase so as to absorb the extra output. Without the required increase in aggregate demand, economic growth might be brought to a stuttering halt because of insufficient spending in the economy. Free-market economists argue that free-market forces automatically generate the extra demand required to absorb extra output. However, Keynesian economists disagree, arguing that if people save too much of their incomes, the incentive to produce the extra output may not be there. In this situation, demand-side policies (expansionary fiscal and/or monetary policy) may be needed to generate the extra required demand. If this is the case, used wisely, demand-side and supply-side policies are best regarded as complementary policies rather than as substitutes for each other. Neither policy should be regarded as always more important than the other.   **25/25 marks**

✒ This is an excellent answer that shows a deep understanding of supply-side economics and supply-side policies, together with an implied understanding of demand-side policies. Analysis and evaluation are very good throughout the answer, which is completed by a final paragraph that justifies the conclusion drawn. It would be hard to see how a better answer could be written amongst the stresses and strains of the exam room, and given the time constraint. Definitely a Level 5 answer; I have awarded full marks.

Scored 35/40   87.5% = middle A* grade

Question 3 The benefits and costs of globalisation

(1) Explain the main features of globalisation. (15 marks)

(2) Evaluate the view that everybody benefits from globalisation. (25 marks)

■ ■ ■

Candidate's answer

(1) Globalisation is the name given to the processes that integrate all or most of the world's economies, making countries increasingly dependent upon each other. Globalisation has been made possible by improvements in information and communication technology (ICT), as well as by developments in more traditional forms of technology. These include massive improvements in passenger air flights and containerisation which has greatly reduced the cost of shifting freight around the world. Examples of globalisation include service industries in the UK dealing with customers through call centres in India, and fashion companies designing their products in Europe, making them in south-east Asia and finally selling most of them in North America.

Two of the main features of globalisation are:
- The growth of international trade and the reduction of trade barriers — a process encouraged by the World Trade Organization (WTO). Globalisation involves the liberalising or freeing-up of world trade. As a result of successive rounds of tariff reduction started in the 1940s, import duties have fallen. This allows specialisation and trade to take place in accordance with the principle of comparative advantage, which in turn increases production and consumption possibilities for most of the different countries in the global economy.
- Greater international mobility of capital and to some extent of labour. Globalisation enables the movement of capital from developed economies to poor economies. In theory it also leads to labour mobility in the opposite direction. However, immigration controls slow down the movement of labour from poor to rich countries. Nevertheless, in recent years illegal immigration into developed economies has occurred because rich countries have informally encouraged migrants to fill the relatively low-paid jobs rejected by their own citizens.

In summary, some of the other features of globalisation are:
- a significant increase in the power of international capitalism and multinational corporations (MNCs) or transnational companies

- the deindustrialisation of older industrial regions and countries, and the movement of manufacturing industries to newly industrialised countries (NICs)
- more recently, the movement of internationally mobile service industries, such as call centres and accounts offices, to NICs
- a decrease in governmental power to influence decisions made by MNCs to shift economic activity between countries **13/15 marks**

🖉 The candidate clearly understands what globalisation is, defines the concept and explains two of the main features of the process. Having done this, he then lists four other characteristics of globalisation but does not really explain them. Overall, his answer falls just short of full marks, which require explanation of a third feature of globalisation.

(2) Free-market economists generally support globalisation and regard its growth as inevitable. They argue that the benefits of further global economic integration, which include the extension of political freedom and democracy as well as the economic benefits of more production and higher living standards, significantly exceed the disadvantages, such as the destruction of local cultures. However, opponents argue that globalisation is a respectable name for the growing exploitation of the poor, mostly in developing countries, by international capitalism and US economic and cultural imperialism.

For its critics, low-paid workers in sweatshops, farmers in the developing world being forced to grow genetically modified crops, the privatisation of state-owned industry to qualify for IMF and World Bank loans, and the growing dominance of US corporate culture and multinational companies symbolise what is wrong with globalisation. According to this view, which I hold myself, globalisation has led to a 'McDonaldisation' or 'Coca-Colonisation' of significant parts of the world's economy. This has involved and continues to involve the destruction of local and national products, identities and cultures by US world brands. The opposite process of 'glocalisation' or local action, is needed to prevent or offset the damage done by globalisation to vulnerable local cultures. Supporters of globalisation counter by arguing that people in the rest of the world demand US products because they consider them superior to traditional local produce.

Another feature of globalisation that has been criticised is the alleged treatment of local labour by multinational corporations. Companies such as Nike have been accused of selling trainers and footballs in developed countries such as the UK at prices far above the cost of raw materials and the low wages paid to Third World labour making the goods. But in response, the multinationals argue that the low wages they pay far exceed the local wages paid by firms indigenous to the countries in which they manufacture. They believe this encourages local wages to rise. MNCs also claim to improve health and safety and other labour market conditions in the poor countries in which they operate.

essay question

But by threatening to close down factories and to move production to poor countries, it is argued that MNCs also reduce wages and living standards in First World countries. Whether this is true depends, of course, on the type of jobs that emerge in developed countries to replace those lost through deindustrialisation and globalisation. Are the new jobs created in the highly skilled service sector, or are they menial, low-paid, unskilled 'McJobs'?

In recent decades, globalisation has considerably reduced the power of national governments, certainly in smaller countries, to control multinational firms operating within their boundaries. National governments have also lost much of the freedom to undertake the economic policies of their choice with respect to managing domestic economies. Governments enjoy less freedom to introduce tariffs and other import controls. At the same time, capital flows into and out of currencies severely constrain a government's ability to implement an independent monetary policy, even when the country's exchange rate is freely floating. **19/25 marks**

In many ways this is a very good answer. Indeed, at least some of the answer could have been included in the answer to Part (1) to pick up the extra marks needed there for explanation. However, although containing lots of relevant knowledge and argument, the answer does not reach Level 5. This is because the candidate has not directly addressed a key word in the question: 'everybody'. Obviously, not everybody gains from globalisation. The answer needs to indicate who the winners and losers are from the globalisation process. There is some implicit debate of this issue, which enables the answer to reach Level 4. Winners and losers may of course vary, depending on the state of the global economy and of individual nation states within the global economy. In the 2008 global recession, it was fashionable to argue that more and more losers were emerging. Also, the recession led to a fall in world trade and in capital flows between countries, along with a move towards greater protectionism. Some commentators argued that de-globalisation processes were replacing those of globalisation. Resumption of global economic growth should, however, reverse this process.

Scored 32/40   80% = low A* grade

 **PHILIP ALLAN**
UPDATES